AN ESSAY ON FACTS

CSLI
Lecture Notes
Number 6

AN ESSAY ON FACTS

Kenneth Russell Olson

CSLI CENTER FOR THE STUDY
OF LANGUAGE
AND INFORMATION

CSLI was founded early in 1983 by researchers from Stanford University, SRI International, and Xerox PARC to further research and development of integrated theories of language, information, and computation. CSLI headquarters and the publication offices are located at the Stanford site.

CSLI/SRI International
333 Ravenswood Avenue
Menlo Park, CA 94025

CSLI/Stanford
Ventura Hall
Stanford, CA 94305

CSLI/Xerox PARC
3333 Coyote Hill Road
Palo Alto, CA 94304

Library of Congress Catalog Card Number: 86-72171
ISBN 0-937073-07-5 (Cloth)
ISBN 0-937073-08-3 (Paper)

Printed in the United States

To John Perry

Contents

Preface

I wish to thank Jon Barwise and Michael Bratman, both of whom made suggestions that led to improvements in the final draft, which had already benefited from discussions with Barwise at various stages along the way.

I owe a special debt to John Perry. Many of the ideas contained here are the product of discussions with him, and are as much his as they are mine. The idea of looking to Bradley for an argument for the existence of facts was, as I recall, entirely Perry's, and is now the keystone of the essay as a whole. His work with Barwise on situation semantics was the immediate impetus for my looking into facts in the first place, and without his encouragement, I might not have persevered.

I also wish to thank Anthony Ungar who read the whole dissertation and provided helpful advice.

Dikran Karagueuzian furnished valuable editorial assistance.

The Center for the Study of Language and Information provided an exciting and stimulating research environment where some of the ideas presented in this work reached their maturity.

Finally, I wish to thank my parents for their support and patience.

Introduction

Flower in the crannied wall,
I pluck you out of the crannies;—
Hold you here, root and all in my hand,
Little flower—but if I could understand
What you are, root and all, and all in all,
I should know what God and man is.

Alfred, Lord Tennyson

Die Welt zerfällt in Tatsachen.
Eines kann der Fall sein oder nicht der Fall sein
und alles übrige gleich bleiben.

Ludwig Wittgenstein

One of the things you sometimes hear philosophers saying is that we are "imprisoned in our conceptual scheme." By this they mean that because we are the kind of beings we are we cannot help but think in terms of certain categories, e.g., thing and property. Other sorts of beings might use different categories, ones just as good as ours, but we are in principle incapable of even imagining them. Evidence of a sort is provided by the difficulty of coming up with any alternatives to the usual categories, though this might equally be taken as supporting a kind of naive realism, according to which our categories, the ones we in fact employ, copy the structure of reality. Neither view makes for very exciting metaphysics. Indeed, they both make for roughly the same one, though the former salves its conscience by labelling it "descriptive." Of course, if there were compelling reasons to consider either of these views true, we should no doubt have to look elsewhere for excitement. Since this does not seem to be the case, however, we can hardly be blamed for wanting to explore alternatives to the standard categories.

What drew me to facts is that they have actually been put forward as such an alternative, most notably by Wittgenstein when he said that the world is the totality of facts, not things. A similar claim could be made on behalf of events; after all, didn't Whitehead hold that things are "adjectives" of events? It seemed to me, however, that the notion of an event is not sufficiently general to serve as a basic ontological category in its own right. Events can be construed either as thinglike or as factlike, and in either case it is only their relation to time that sets them apart as a special case. But what Whitehead claimed about events could equally well be claimed about facts in general. Individuals, properties, and relations can be conceived of as adjectives of events because events seem to comprise these elements in themselves. But they do so only if they are construed as a kind of fact.

The first question I asked myself was what reason could be given for admitting fact as a metaphysical category in its own right. The answer that facts are needed for true sentences to correspond to seemed to me an obvious non-starter. For the notion of correspondence to have any teeth, we must suppose that the words of the sentence match constituents of the fact. But it is naive to suppose that the way language presents things has any such direct relation to the way things really are. If, on the other hand, we drop the notion of correspondence for that of "fitting," it is far from clear that it is facts rather than things that sentences fit. It is the white snow itself that makes the sentence "snow is white" true, never mind that snow is not "articulated" the way the sentence is.

Besides, it would be absurd to go around positing metaphysical categories merely to explain such human phenomena as language and belief.

I could think of only one reason to deny that the world is the totality of things, and that was the existence of relations. It is natural to think of a thing's properties as inhering in it, so that once we have all the things we have all their properties as well. In contrast, it is not at all natural to think of relations in this way, as the controversy about internal relations serves to indicate. Once we add relations, then, things no longer tell the whole story. In addition to the cup and the saucer we have to take account of the fact that the cup is on the saucer.

This also seemed to explain why facts appeared so late on the philosophical scene, viz, in the latter half of the nineteenth century. For at this time relations were also starting to come into their own. It took a certain amount of digging to confirm this hunch. From this point of view, Russell and Wittgenstein proved somewhat disappointing since, at the time they were writing, facts and relations could be taken more or less for granted. But in Mill, Peirce, and especially Bradley, I found confirmation exceeding my expectations.

My approach will be as follows. First, I remind the reader of some distinctions without which clarity about facts, whether there be such or not, is impossible to achieve. After that, I tell the story of the pressures that led to the concept. Then I move into a discussion of arguments for and against.

In Chapter 1, I contrast facts with propositions, arguing that the two notions are farther apart than is generally assumed. In my opinion, it is extremely important to realize that the notion of a fact is a metaphysical one, whereas that of a proposition has its home in semantics. The contrast is especially clear when the proposition is construed as a Fregean thought, since it will then have as constituents senses referring to things rather than things themselves. Not just particulars, but even properties and relations, must be distinguished from the senses referring to them. Nor is this is just a peculiarity of Frege's theory, since concepts in general have different identity criteria than properties. Whenever we can make a discrimination or understand an expression it is reasonable to suppose that we have a corresponding concept. I argue that we should be less free in positing properties. Facts, unlike propositions, are made up of the various things, properties, and relations themselves, not concepts of them. To be sure, this would also be true of propositions, as Russell conceived of propositions. On this view, there seems to be no difference between facts and true propositions. But in order to serve as objects of belief and meanings of sentences, propositions must nevertheless be more finely individuated than it is reasonable to suppose that facts are. The things, properties, and relations must be taken more or less as they are given by language. I conclude the chapter with the hypothesis about facts and relations mentioned above.

Chapter 2 is chiefly historical. I begin by discussing the role of relations in the Aristotelian tradition, which represents the most thorough working out to date of the view that the world is a totality of things as opposed to, say, facts. When Aristotle and the Scholastics talk of relations they mean relational *properties*. The things related are divided into subject and term, and the relation is held to *inhere* in the subject, as opposed to holding *between* subject and term, as Russell has taught us to view it. This led to a kind of metaphysical version of action at a distance, since it was recognized that sometimes the subject acquired or lost such a property purely as a result of the vicissitudes of the term, as when a thing becomes smaller than another without changing in size, through the growth of the latter. This is one kind of situation that occasioned talk of the "foundation" of a relation, the basis for asserting that the relation holds. In this case, it consists in the sizes of the things related. In the language of facts, the doctrine can be expressed by saying that we call the one greater than the other because of a quite definite fact about their respective sizes, e.g., that the one is three feet tall and the other is four feet tall. The Scholastics did not have the notion of a fact, but had to make do with those of substance and attribute. In the present case, they said that there are two foundations, one a property in the subject and the other a property in the term. But in the nineteenth century the doctrine was taken up by Mill and Peirce and applied explicitly to facts. The foundation of a relation was now some concrete fact about the subject and term which suffices to make the relational claim true. For example, the relation between hen and chick consists in the fact that the one laid the egg out of which the other was hatched. It is this fact, and not the relation, that is metaphysically basic. Mill thought that he had succeeded in giving a nominalistic reduction of relations, while Peirce espoused a subtle form of realism. Both took themselves to be expounding the scholastic notion, but I argue that they were mistaken about this.

The best argument I know of for the existence of facts is due to Bradley. This is the famous regress argument, and it is the subject of Chapter 3. The regress argument is usually interpreted as an argument against relations. Bradley certainly uses it to relegate relations to the realm of *appearance* as opposed to reality, but it would be a mistake—admittedly, a rather natural one—to suppose that by this he meant that there are no relations. Appearance and reality are a matter of degree, according to him, and to call something appearance is roughly to say that it exists as an aspect of a concrete whole. In the case of relations, this whole is what he calls the "relational situation," a concrete fact such as the wolf's eating the lamb. In other words, his position is similar to that of Mill and Peirce. The burden of the regress argument is to show that such relational facts, which certainly exist prima facie, cannot be reduced to the terms and relations which are their constituents. I state the argument and defend it against various objections.

In Chapter 4, I discuss the argument *against* facts that Barwise and Perry have dubbed "the slingshot." This argument was adumbrated by Frege in "On Sense and Reference," where it serves as a justification for regarding truth values as the references of sentences, in place of the fact-like entities that had played this role in his previous writings. I adduce evidence to show that this, and not the well-known puzzle regarding identity, is what led to the distinction between sense and reference in the first place. Thoughts had to be introduced because truth values are not finely individuated enough to serve as objects of belief. The distinction between sense and reference, having thus been made on the level of sentences, trickled down to their parts (in what might be termed "Fregenomics"). The slingshot received its first explicit formulation from Church and was subsequently used by Davidson, but perhaps the most instructive version is due to Gödel. After considering various formulations and the objections that have been raised against them, I conclude that the argument does not disprove the existence of facts, but that in order to say why it does not we are forced to choose between two rival conceptions of their nature, which, modifying a terminology due to Fine, I call the "structuralist" and the "existentialist" conceptions. According to the former, facts are structured entities, and fact A is the same as fact B only if it consists of the same objects in the same relations. According to the latter, fact A is the same as fact B if they necessarily coexist. The existentialist conception is obviously more compatible with the idea that facts are basic, which I cautiously endorse.

Chapter 1

Separating Fact from Fiction

Facts and Propositions

New ideas about first philosophy are always in short supply. For the most part, the history of the subject has consisted of variations on the theme of things and their properties. If for "things" and "properties" we read "participants" and "forms," we may begin to see the justice, in this limited sphere at least, of Whitehead's remark that philosophers have all along only been footnoting Plato.

Towards the end of the last century, however, some of them were engaged in breaking new ground. Among the fruits of their labor were the notions of relation and fact. Our subject is the latter, though, as we shall see, the two are not unconnected. Relations had previously been viewed with distrust. Facts, on the other hand, were almost a complete novelty. At any rate, Russell (1971) presented them as such in his "Philosophy of Logical Atomism":

> The first thing I want to emphasize is that the outer world—the world, so to speak, which knowledge is aiming at knowing—is not completely described by a lot of "particulars," but that you must also take account of these things that I call facts, which are the sort of things that you express by a sentence, and that these, just as much as particular chairs and tables, are part of the real world. (183)

Facts belong—almost literally, as we see here—to the "furniture of the universe" (hence, perhaps, the phrase "unvarnished facts"), to the world itself, and not merely to the apparatus by means of which we represent it. It is chiefly this that separates them from those other alleged entities, propositions, which are so often mentioned in the same breath with facts and are likewise described by their devotees as the sort of things expressed by sentences. For no one would ever have thought of propositions except in connection with language or belief. Facts, on the other hand, would have made themselves felt even if we confined our attention to inanimate nature. The other differences between facts and propositions all issue from this one.

Propositions arise as objects of belief or meanings of sentences or both. Inevitably, then, they are divided into true and false. There is no corresponding division of facts. False sentences do not express facts; *that*, we are tempted to say, is what makes them false. Some philosophers would say that they express possible facts. That may be. But merely possible facts are no more a species of fact than merely possible persons are a species of person. Possible facts are sometimes called "states of affairs."

Facts are usually regarded as complex. Their constituents, like themselves, are parts of the real world, and include things, properties, and relations. For example, the fact that this paper is white is composed of the paper itself and the property of being white. And propositions? On one view, they are composed of the same sorts of things as facts are. Thus the proposition that the earth is flat would be made up of the earth itself and the property of being flat. Moore seems to have been the first to take such a view of propositions, and for a time it was shared by Russell. A somewhat older view is that propositions are made up, not of the things themselves, but of *concepts* of them. The word "concept" has psychological overtones, but I shall use it to refer to something abstract, viz, a *way* of conceiving of something that may be shared by several people.

The first formulation of this view in modern philosophy is Bolzano's theory of "sentences in themselves" (*Saetze an sich*), which are composed according to him of "ideas in themselves" (*Vorstellungen an sich*), the point of the phrase "in themselves" being to cancel the linguistic connotations of "sentence" and the psychological ones of "idea." Sentences in themselves are not sentences at all, but rather the meanings thereof. They also serve as objects of judgment. Before Bolzano, there was no clear distinction between the act of judging, which is unsharable and unrepeatable, and the content judged, which may be the same in different acts.

The classical account, however, is Frege's theory of sense and reference, according to which a sentence *refers to* a truth value—an object called the True in the case of true sentences and the False in the case of false ones—and *expresses* what he calls a "thought," which is his term for a proposition. The relation between a thought and its truth value is that of a concept to the object to which it applies. Thus the sentence "Aristotle was a Greek" expresses a concept of the True, just as "the teacher of Alexander" expresses a concept of Aristotle. The concepts expressed by the parts of a sentence are parts of the thought expressed by the sentence as a whole. Both the thought and its component concepts are called "senses."[1] The distinction between sense and reference extends to predicates as well as to singular terms. For the time being we may think of a predicate like "is a Greek" as standing for the class of things of which it is true.[2] If we do so, we may regard the sense of a predicate, like that of a singular term, as a concept. The only difference is that whereas the sense of "Aristotle" is an individual concept, with uniqueness of reference built in, that of "is Greek" is a class concept.

The notion of a concept is often confused with that of a property, but as *notions* at any rate they are distinct, being defined in different ways. Properties *belong* to things and are responsible for their similarities and differences. Concepts, whether of classes or of individuals, are ways in which we conceive of things.[3] This is not to say that concepts are mental entities, like sensations. The term "concept" has a long history of ambiguity, being used now in an abstract, now in a psychological sense, even by the same author. I am using it in the abstract sense: concepts are *ways* of conceiving of things, and as such they can be shared by different minds. My point is that even when so regarded concepts are different from

---

[1] Senses are concepts as *we* have been using the term "concept," but not as Frege uses it. But it is his use that is deviant, not ours. Even Church, who follows Frege's terminology closely in other respects, refers to senses as concepts of the objects to which they apply. For Frege's use of "concept," see the next footnote.

[2] In fact it stands, according to Frege, for what would nowadays be called the "characteristic function" of this class, i.e., a function that gives the True as value for members of the class and the False for non-members. Such a function is what Frege himself called a "concept" (*Begriff*), distinguishing it both from the sense, on the one hand, and from the "extension" (*Umfang*) of the concept, on the other. Even the extension of the concept is not exactly a class, but rather what he calls a "course of values," which bears some resemblance to the ordinary notion of the extension of a function as a set of ordered pairs, without, however, being identical with it. Part of the problem is that Frege's notion of a function does not quite square with any current one. The subject is further discussed in Chapter 4.

[3] Since it is here a question of what we *mean* by the two terms, grammatical evidence may not be altogether out of place. The phrases "properties of matter" and "concepts of matter" seem to be on a par. But the former admits of the paraphrase "matter's properties," whereas the latter cannot be paraphrased by "matter's concept's," a phrase which suggests that matter thinks, no doubt about Vienna. I believe that the phrase "concepts of matter" is what grammarians used to call an objective, as opposed to a possessive, genitive. It is like "pictures of animals."

properties. Reference to mind is inseparable from the notion of a concept, but it plays no part in that of a property.

The assimilation of properties to concepts is perhaps mostly inadvertent, arising from a simple failure to distinguish them. But it may also arise from the belief that one of these notions can do the work of both. In both cases it is abetted by preoccupation with the question of extensionality. One philosopher who makes the identification with open eyes is Church (1956):

> A property, as ordinarily understood, differs from a class only or chiefly in that two properties may be different though the classes determined by them are the same (where the class determined by a property is the class whose members are the things that have that property). Therefore, we identify a property with a class concept, or concept of a class. (30)

The implicit premise here is that class concepts, too, differ from classes only or chiefly in that two of them may determine the same class. Hence they are either identical with properties or may safely be treated as if they were. The one distinction that must be observed is between entities that satisfy the principle of extensionality and ones that do not.

It seems to me that extensionality neither constitutes nor explains the difference between classes and properties. For if these really are different, it stands to reason that they would be so even in a world in which no two properties determined the same class. Its significance lies rather in showing that they are different. For if classes and properties were the same, then the mapping that assigns to each property the class of things that have it would be an identity map. But since classes satisfy the principle of extensionality and properties do not, this mapping is not even one to one. Hence, classes cannot be properties. Nor, by the same token, can they be concepts.

The distinctness of properties and concepts admits of no such clear and irrefragable proof. But that does not make it any the less real. Both properties and concepts are said to *determine* classes. But, prima facie at any rate, the determining relation is not the same in the two cases. A property determines the class of things that *have* it; a concept, the class it *represents*. As we shall see, moreover, it is at least plausible to suppose that concepts are more finely individuated than properties, just as the latter are more finely individuated than sets.

The doctrine that properties are nothing but *mental* concepts is known traditionally as conceptualism. It is really nominalism in psychological guise and is prompted like the latter by an aversion to universals. The standard objection to it is that it makes a mystery of our applying a concept to one thing and not another. The conceptualist can hardly appeal to the properties of the two things, since, according to him, to say that two things have different properties is just to say that we apply different concepts to them. Making the concepts abstract rather than mental does not affect the argument, which does not depend on the subjectivity of concepts. But since abstract concepts can be shared by different minds they must themselves be accounted a species of universal, the very thing the traditional conceptualist was out to avoid. Hence the view that properties are concepts in the abstract sense combines the worst of both worlds.

The reverse approach—identifying concepts with properties—may initially look more promising. On this view, what we "grasp" when we understand a predicate like "is white" is the property itself, in this case the property of being white. But it too is exposed to objections. First, there is Russell's antinomy of impredicable properties, which is similar to his earlier and much more famous paradox about classes. A property is called "impredicable" if it does not exemplify itself. For example, the property of being white would be impredicable, since properties are not colored, while that of being a property would not, since it is itself a property. A contradiction is obtained in the obvious way by asking whether the property of being impredicable exemplifies itself. This strongly suggests that there is no such property as that of being impredicable. A fortiori, then, it is not by "grasping" this property that we understand the expression "is impredicable." Yet understand it we do, since otherwise we should be unable to follow the argument.

A similar lesson may be drawn from Wittgenstein's well known discussion of games in the *Philosophical Investigations.* Wittgenstein attempts to show, by dint of many and various examples, that there is no single property common to all the things we call "games." Instead, some are alike in one respect, others in another, like the members of a family. Our ability to tell members from non-members argues our possession of a concept. But this concept cannot be the *property* of being a game; for if Wittgenstein is right there is no such property. And he clearly thinks that games are not alone in this respect.[4]

A closer look thus tends to uphold the prima facie distinction between properties and concepts. The former belong to the world itself; the latter to our representation of it (which is not to say that they are only in the mind).

---

[4] Indeed, Wittgenstein is often taken as denying that there *are* properties, and his doctrine of "family resemblance" regarded as a "solution to the problem of universals." Both these claims seem to me to be exaggerated. The various respects in which members of a family resemble each other will still need to be admitted as universals, or at least the relation of resemblance itself will, as Russell argued in a different context.

One consequence of this is the relative difficulty of establishing the existence of a property as opposed to that of a mere concept. By and large, every predicate expresses a concept. We have seen that they do not all express properties. The supposition that they do—besides running afoul of the objections raised above—offends against the same sense of reality that Russell urged in opposition to Meinong. The question what properties there are can no more be settled by appealing to language than can the same question regarding things. Both are—in large part at least—empirical questions.[5]

Similar remarks apply to facts themselves, since they are composed of things and properties. We already know that not every sentence expresses a fact: no false one does. But what about true sentences? On the one hand, according to the correspondence theory, truth just *is* agreement with fact. The prospect of defining truth directly in this way has been an abiding incentive for positing facts. For example, the sentence "this paper is white" is true in virtue of matching up with the fact that this paper is white, which consists of this paper and the property of being white. So far, so good. It is not implausible that there should be such a fact and that the sentence in question should correspond to it. But how about the sentence "Super Bowl XVI was a game?" This sentence is true enough, but what fact makes it so? That Super Bowl XVI was a game? But what fact is this? Not, surely, the fact consisting of Super Bowl XVI and the *property* of being a game. For we have reason to think that there is no such property, even granting that there is such a thing as Super Bowl XVI. But if some other fact or facts make this sentence true, then it is only in a somewhat attenuated sense that it may be said to correspond to them.

So far we have confined our attention to subject-predicate sentences. Relational sentences pose no additional problems, important as they will prove to be in other respects. But what of all the other forms of sentence, negations, conjunctions, and the rest? From what has been said already, we should be wary of positing corresponding forms of fact. One argument against doing so is the interdefinability of the logical constants: surely sentences related as, say, "not-(p or q)" and "(not-p or not-q)" express the same fact, if any. We can get around this particular example by admitting either conjunctive or disjunctive facts, but not both. But if we stick to our

---

[5] The chief advocate of such a position has been Armstrong (1978), who would in fact say that they are questions for *science*. But as Grossmann (1983, 151) points out, we can take an empirical approach to properties without embracing Armstrong's "scientism." Grossmann himself emphasizes the possibility of perceiving properties directly. It seems to me rather that both properties *and* things are theoretical, as opposed to observational entities, but that the theory in question need not be "scientific" in any useful sense of the word.

realism about facts, this choice cannot just be a matter of convention; it requires justification. A problem with all such facts is saying what they are without relying in an essential way on the sentences that express them. This can be done in the case of atomic facts, assuming there are such, by referring to their constituents. Such a fact consists in a thing's exemplifying a property or two things' standing in a relation, etc. But what of conjunctive facts? One approach is to suppose that the word "and" stands for a relation between facts. A conjunctive fact would then consist in two facts' standing in this relation. In the case of disjunctive facts, however, even this rather jejune expedient is unavailable; for if only one disjunct is true, then the other does not express a fact at all, and so there will be only the one fact and not two as required by the relation. Russell, as we shall see, argued in favor of negative and general facts, but drew the line at conjunctive and disjunctive ones, in part because he could not bring himself to believe in reified "ands" and "ors." And even in the case of negative and general facts, he admitted that he lacked a satisfactory analysis.

We would do well to be suspicious of "entities" cloned from linguistic expressions. Set theory is especially fecund in such entities, because of its apparently limitless ability to mimic structure. Some of them may occasionally be useful for purposes of semantic bookkeeping, but it would be a mistake to regard them as metaphysically fundamental. Their claim to reality rings hollow when they cleave too closely to language. This may seem to overlook the fact that language is itself a representation of the world, and a highly successful one. Austin remarks somewhere that ordinary language contains a metaphysics that has been refined continuously over time and is thus likely to be better than anything a philosopher could come up with in an afternoon. Perhaps we are justified after all in inferring the structure of facts from sentences, since sentences have had so long to conform themselves to facts. As we shall see presently, Austin himself did not draw this conclusion. And it would surely be wrong for us to do so. If the grammatical structure of our language, as opposed to its vocabulary, incorporates a metaphysics at all, it is more likely to be the substance-attribute metaphysics, which is so often laid at its doorstep, e.g., by Russell, than one incorporating the notion of a fact, which made such a late entrance on the philosophical stage. This is not to deny that sentences are *true* in virtue of facts. But *that* they are is a philosophical theory, not something built into the grammar of our language. A sentence as a whole does not purport to stand for anything, but only to make a statement *about* something. In view of this it would be quite fortuitous if there were anything like a one to one correspondence between facts and sentences.[6] Russell's

[6] Further reasons for thinking that there is not will be found in Chapter 4.

view of ordinary language is a useful corrective to Austin's: he said that it "embodies the superstitions of cannibals."

Be that as it may, I wish not to bury Austin but to praise him. For the view I want to maintain, viz, that true statements fit the facts but do not necessarily fit them like a glove, was first put forward by him. Or at least he went further in this direction than his predecessors, since he emphasized that a statement's fitting the facts is not an all-or-nothing affair. One fit may be better than another, and in some cases there may be no such thing as a perfect fit. This idea may be hard to incorporate into a formal semantics, but it has the merit of recognizing the great abyss that separates language and reality. One place Austin made use of it was in his debate with Strawson. The latter had claimed that facts are not really "in the world" the way things, persons, and events are. According to him, it is vacuous to say that a true statement is one that fits the facts, because facts are really *arti*facts of language. To what fact does the statement that it is raining correspond? Why, to the *fact* that it is raining, of course! But this answer is straight out of Moliere. "Of course statements and facts fit," said Strawson. "They were made for each other."

If facts really were "wedded to that-clauses" as closely as Strawson claims, their reality would indeed be suspect. But this is precisely what Austin denies. Characteristically, he appeals to linguistic evidence, in this case the history of the word "fact" as recorded in the *Oxford English Dictionary.* Since I plan to cover some of the same ground in the next section, I shall mention here only his main point, which is that by the eighteenth century "fact" had already come to mean in general what it means today, i.e., "something that is the case." Only later, and in dependence on this meaning, was the phrase "fact that" introduced, and then only as a convenient alternative to gerundial constructions where the latter were felt to be awkward. Consequently, "to explain the meaning of 'fact' in terms of the expression 'fact that' is to invert the real order of things." (112) Austin is not just making a philological point. Nor, on the other hand, is he naively arguing that the world must be a certain way on the basis of etymology. He is rather trying to show that our *concept* of a fact is not parasitic upon that-clauses in the way Strawson maintains. The dictionary comes in as an alternative to mere introspection: since people spoke of facts before anyone coined the phrase "fact that," the concept of the former can hardly depend on the latter. As Austin sees it, the phrase in question is actually rather specialized in its application:

> 'Fact that' is a phrase designed for use in situations where the distinction between a true statement and the state of affairs about which it is a truth is neglected; as it often is with advantage in

> ordinary life, though seldom in philosophy—above all in discussing truth, where it is precisely our business to prise the words off the world and keep them off it. (92)

In other words, when we talk about "the fact that *S*" we are not just talking about the fact, but about "*S*" as well, just as we are talking about "Gorgione" as well as Gorgione in Quine's example "Gorgione was so-called because of his size." Use of the phrase, according to Austin, "is a compendious way of speaking about a situation involving both words and world." This is why it is such a platitude to say that "*S*" corresponds to the fact that *S*.[7] Even the word "corresponds" is misleading, since it suggests too great a parallelism between sentence and fact, when their relation may be purely a matter of convention:

> There is no need whatsoever for the words used in making a true statement to 'mirror' in any way, however indirect, any feature whatsoever of the situation or event; a statement no more needs, in order to be true, to reproduce the 'multiplicity,' say, or the 'structure' or 'form' of the reality, than a word needs to be echoic or pictographic. To suppose that it does, is to fall once again into the error of reading back into the world the features of language. (93)

This might sound odd coming from a linguistic philosopher, especially Austin, given his views about language and metaphysics mentioned above. But it fits in well with another theme of his writings, viz, the multifariousness of the devices—or crotchets, as the case may be—with which language operates.[8]

When Russell said that facts are the sort of things that we express by a sentence, he meant that they are the sort of things that are the *case*. The reference to sentences was by way of elucidation, not definition, much as if he had said that cats are the sort of things dogs like to chase. According to

---

[7] Vendler, who claims that Austin was "napping" when he said that some facts are events, appears to have nodded off during the latter's remarks about that-clauses. For his own argument depends on linking the use of the word "fact" to what he calls "perfect nominals," of which such clauses are the most prominent examples.

[8] Austin also emphasizes the role of non-verbal demonstrative devices in determining what fact a given statement is aiming to fit. In general, sentences correspond not to individual facts, but to *types* of facts. Thus, by itself, the phrase "the fact that *S*" may not refer to a unique fact at all. As we shall see in Chapter 3, this idea goes back to Bradley. It has recently been made precise by Barwise and Perry.

Russell, the notion of a fact is basic and undefinable. As we have seen, its home is in metaphysics, not semantics. The opposite is true of propositions, which were born of sentences and cannot do their job if they lose contact with them. (This is why their identification with sets of possible worlds is felt to be unsatisfactory.) Propositions are thus caught in a double bind. They have to march in step with language, but this very fact prejudices their claim to ultimate reality.

Getting Down to Brass Tacks

According to Fowler's *Modern English Usage*, the phrase "brass tacks" originated as Cockney rhyming slang for "facts," like "apples and pears" for "stairs" or "Cain and Abel" for "table," a colorful reminder that the word "fact" was in common use long before philosophers got hold of it. This is yet another way in which facts differ from propositions. "Fact" derives from the Latin *factum*, meaning "thing done," itself the neuter past participle of *facere*, "to do or make."[9] The English word, too, originally had the sense of deed or action, more often than not criminal. (The word "feat," which is also derived from *factum*—by way of the Old French *fait*—retains the original sense of something done.) Its meaning was thence extended to include, among other things:

(1) occurrences *in general*, as well as actions; hence

(2) what *is the case*, whether an occurrence or not; hence

(3) what is *known* to be the case; hence

(4) what is known by *observation*, rather than inference; hence

(5) the actual *data* of experience, as opposed to what we infer; and, developing out of one or more of the above senses,

(6) actually existing *things*, such as persons and institutions, apparently to contrast them with fictions (a use the dictionary characterizes as "strained").

The notion of fact with which we are concerned is closer to (2) than to any of the others. But these are all of them ordinary uses of the word, not philosophical ones. Certainly none of them commits the user to facts as entities in their own right. It follows that even a philosopher may use the word "fact" without talking about facts. This will prove to be true even when the term figures prominently in his writings and is employed in a

[9] The etymological information presented here is culled from the *Oxford English Dictionary*, s.v. "Fact."

technical or quasi-technical sense. Thus the very fact that "fact" is so well established in ordinary language poses a problem for anyone interested in the history of the concept. We are not just looking for writers who use the word "fact" or its cognates, but for ones who use it in a particular way.

The Scholastics already used the Latin word *factum* in one or more of the extended senses above, which have also passed to its Romance derivatives. They also used the expression *res facti* for a thing that exists or is known to exist. But none of them posited facts as entities *sui generis*, so far as I am aware, and we shall see in the next chapter why none is likely to have done so.

In modern times we find Leibniz using *fait* in the phrase *verites de fait*. But his ontology had no more room for facts than did that of the Scholastics. In like manner, Hume wrote of "matters of fact" (translating the scholastic *res facti*), but not of "facts" by themselves. To be sure, he defines (contingent) truth as correspondence to matters of fact. Since this is the same role facts themselves play in later theories it begins to look as if matters of fact are just facts under another name. But this is belied by the fact that in the later theories it is always a sentence or complete thought that is said to correspond, whereas Hume takes the correspondence to be between ideas and individual things. He may, however, be held responsible for forging a link between facts and contingency with his distinction between matters of fact and relations of ideas. Many would regard the phrase "necessary fact" as an oxymoron.

According to Eisler, the German word *Tatsache* (s.v.) was introduced by Herder in the eighteenth century as a more or less literal translation for Hume's "matter of fact." And until Wittgenstein got hold of it in the twentieth it seems to have been applied, like its English counterpart, mainly to things, not facts. According to Kant, *Tatsachen* are "Gegenstände für Begriffe, deren objektive Realität (es sei durch reine Vernunft oder durch Erfahrung und, im ersteren Falle, aus theoretischen oder praktischen Datis derselben, in allen Fällen aber vermittelst einer ihnen korrespondierenden Anschauung) bewiesen werden kann." This, with its emphasis on *Anschauung*, perhaps comes closest to sense (4) in the above list. Eisler gives a long list of quotations, in which the Neo-Kantians are particularly well represented. But not until we come to a relatively late example from Schlick do we get anything like the notion we are after. For the most part the quotations move back and forth between senses (4) and (5).

Among nineteenth-century British philosophers, Mill and Bradley have the most to say about facts. The former uses the term at least sometimes in our sense (2) of an existent state of affairs, but his usage is not altogether fixed. Sometimes he suggests that facts are, or are analyzable into, physical events, which is sense (1), but this does not seem to be true of all of his examples. As we shall see in the next chapter, he is also the first to make facts do some philosophical work, in connection with relations. I shall defer further discussion of him until then.

Bradley is so important to my story that I have devoted a full chapter to him. The primary sense in which he uses the term "fact" is that conveyed by the following passage:

> A judgment, we assume naturally, says something about some fact or reality. If we asserted or denied about anything else, our judgment would seem to be a frivolous pretence. We must not only say something, but it must be about something actual that we say it. (1950b, 1:41)

The phrase "or reality" in the first sentence is clearly intended as epexegetical. "A fact" and "a reality" mean the same thing for Bradley, as does the "something actual" of the last sentence. We are thus dealing with sense (6). But Bradley deliberately exploits the ambiguity between it and sense (2). According to him, reality is a matter of degree. Something is real to the extent that it contains the conditions for its existence within itself. To the extent that these conditions lie outside of it, it is not a reality but only an abstraction from a larger whole. And since everything ultimately involves everything else, nothing is fully real except the universe as a whole. But among lesser things, some are more real than others. For example, relational facts are more real than the individuals and relations making them up. And everything is of the nature of such a fact, since analysis never yields ultimate simples, but only "pluralities in unity."[10] These somewhat sketchy remarks will be filled out in Chapter 3.

The present survey would be incomplete if it did not include one other nineteenth-century philosopher. Convinced that Aristotle's categories were outdated, Peirce took it upon himself to compose a new list. His categories were but three in number, and although they went by different names at different times, they were always recognizably the same. In a manuscript of around 1896 entitled "The Logic of Mathematics; An Attempt to Develop My Categories From Within," they appear as Quality, Fact, and Law. Peirce calls them "the most universal categories of elements of all experience, natural or poetical" (1, 227) and later says that they are the *only* such

---

[10] Bradley is usually portrayed as unfriendly to facts. Thus Wollheim devotes two chapters of his book on Bradley to "The Case Against Facts," and Austin says that Bradley "had some by no means ill-deserved cold water to pour upon facts, at the crucial point." (109) But it is to facts in the "epistemic" senses (3)–(5) that Bradley objected. As we have seen, Austin certainly did not think facts in general to be in need of such a bath.

(1, 230). This is a surprising short list, as much for what it leaves out as for what it includes. Among the things it leaves out are particulars and relations. The latter omission would scarcely be remarkable were the omitter anyone but Peirce. For philosophers routinely ignored relations or tried to explain them away until Peirce and Russell made them respectable. And it was Peirce who took the first step in this direction by developing the formal logic of relations (though De Morgan had already pointed the way). The omission of particulars would be surprising coming from anyone, since substance had gone unchallenged as *the* fundamental category since Aristotle.

As examples of qualities, Peirce names "red, bitter, tedious, hard, heartrending, noble." (1, 228) A self-styled realist about universals, he insists that they are in no way dependent upon the mind. Nor are they dependent on being exemplified by particulars. The latter view is stigmatized as "the great error of all the nominalistic schools." (1, 230) Peirce equates qualities with potentialities that may or may not be realized.[11] According to Peirce, when we consider *anything* in isolation we are really considering it as potential rather than as actual. Actuality consists in "having a place in the general system of the universe." (1, 232) Peirce is fond of the somewhat Hegelian image of a thing's maintaining itself in the struggle for existence by means of its asymmetrical relations to other individuals. What seems to underlie this picture is a version of the identity of indiscernibles. This table is distinct from another exactly similar table because it stands in different relations to the rest of the world. Take away these relations and we no longer have two tables. Peirce seems to have thought that apart from its relations the table is just a cluster of qualities, or a single complex quality, consisting, e.g., of brownness, woodenness, and rectangularity. Since a thing considered in isolation turns out to be a kind of quality, the category of Quality is associated with the number one, and described as "the monadic element of the world," or Firstness.

By contrast, a typical fact involves two things in relation to one another. It is only in virtue of such facts that we are entitled to speak of things in the first place instead of just qualities. To be sure, there are also facts consisting of a single thing and a property. Peirce calls these inherential, as opposed to relational, facts. But the former are parasitic upon the latter, in that the world could not consist entirely of inherential facts. According to Peirce, there would be nothing to distinguish such a world from a mere set of potentialities, nor any reason for regarding it as one

---

[11] The opposite opinion, that qualities exist only if exemplified at some time or other, is not properly called nominalism, but rather moderate, or Aristotelian, realism. A *nominalist* denies universals altogether. But Peirce may have meant that moderate realism *leads* to nominalism.

world rather than many or none. Actuality therefore makes its appearance together with facts. A thing exists only if it figures in at least one relational fact. On the other hand, relations themselves exist only in so far as there are things that stand in them. In this respect, relations still take a back seat to qualities in Peirce's ontology. For the latter can exist uninstantiated, whereas the former cannot. Things and relations are thus mutually interdependent and occur only in the context of some fact or other. This accounts for the absence of separate categories of Thing and Relation. For Peirce, things and relations are both more or less abstractions from facts. Because there must be dyadic facts if there are to be facts at all, he thinks of Fact as the dyadic element of the world, just as Quality is the monadic. For this reason, he sometimes refers to Fact as Secondness. (1, 233–53)

If inherential facts are facts only by courtesy as it were, even this much is denied those putative facts in which only qualities figure. That scarlet is red is not a fact, according to Peirce. "It is a *truth*; but it is only an essential truth. It is that in being which corresponds to Kant's analytical judgment." (1, 246) He thus assigns it to the category of Quality rather than that of Fact. As he puts it, Fact always involves an element of accident or of brute force. In this respect, it is like Hume's matter of fact.

On another issue Peirce and Hume part company. According to Peirce, the world is not completely described by a lot of facts. We must also take account of what he calls laws. In some respects, laws resemble facts. Both are the sort of things expressed by sentences, for example. Laws are expressed by general statements, but not every general statement expresses a law. For example, "all U.S. presidents are male" presumably does not. Even were it to hold good until the demise of the Republic, it would still be more or less a coincidence. Laws, in contrast to mere regularities, are necessary. They cover not just all actual cases, but all possible ones. (The possibility involved is physical or metaphysical instead of logical, for reasons that should be clear from the above.) With this proviso, laws can be regarded as a species of general fact: "There is no objection to saying that a law is a general fact, provided it be understood that the general has an admixture of potentiality in it, so that no congeries of actions here and now can ever make a general fact." (1, 229) A world in which there are facts, but no laws, might be empirically indistinguishable from one in which there are laws as well, though I am not sure Peirce's pragmatism would let him admit this. The one would be a Humean world, the other one in which causality is more than just constant conjunction. In any case, the distinction seemed fundamental enough to Peirce to warrant elevating Law to the status of a separate category.

The terms of the causal relation are always facts, according to Peirce. One fact causes another if a sentence expressing the latter follows from one expressing the former together with one expressing a law of nature. Because a law thus mediates between two other terms, Peirce regards it as the triadic element of the world. For this reason he sometimes refers to Law as Thirdness.[12]

Pace the Dictionary, (6) seems to have been the standard *philosophical* sense of "fact" at the turn of the century, though not all writers were as careful as Bradley to banish the purely psychological associations emanating from (3)–(5). A handy guide to contemporary usage is Baldwin's *Dictionary of Philosophy and Psychology*, which was published in 1901. The article on "Fact," written by Baldwin and Stout, reads in part as follows:

> Fact might be defined thus: datum of experience considered as abstracted from the experience of which it is a datum. The notion of fact includes abstraction even from the experiences by which the fact is reached or asserted. And inasmuch as it is just this sort of abstraction which the notion of actuality—or of the so-called 'trans-subjective'—covers, we may say that a fact is anything which is found to be actual. The fact is, however, not absolute, but always relative to some experience.

If we make allowances for the authors' psychologism, which makes them view reality as the result of *substracting* something from *experience*, this boils down to the assertion that a fact is something actual, which is sense (6). But the rider seems to undo the subtraction, and we cannot really be sure that we aren't dealing with sense (4) or even sense (5). Incompatible ideas seem to be held in uneasy suspension.

Nevertheless, by the end of the nineteenth century the notion of a fact had clearly come into its own and was about to do so even more in the first decades of the next. Why precisely now and not before? After all, propositions had been around in one form or another for a long time, as Stoic *lekta* and scholastic *complexe significabilia*, not to mention Bolzano's *Saetze an sich* and Frege's *Gedanken*. Yet these are all shadowy half-entities compared to facts. Why do facts appear on the scene so late? Geach gives the following explanation, which may sound familiar:

---

[12] This explanation is obviously somewhat forced. Peirce was more wedded to the idea of trichotomy than to any particular rationale for it. Elsewhere he uses the alleged fact that relations of more than three terms are always reducible to triadic ones to establish three as the magic number. He believed that there are *irreducibly* triadic relations, though his confidence that he could produce an example seems to have been greater at some times than at others. In the paper we are discussing, he maintains that *representation* is irreducibly triadic, involving a sign, an object, and an interpreter. (1, 256)

> Facts came to be counted among the entities in the philosopher's world only after the construction whereby "the fact," or its synonym in another language , is put in opposition with an indirect-statement clause had spread like the pox from one European language to another, largely by way of journalism. This happened at the turn of the last century; only then did philosophers come to postulate facts as individual entities, answering to the phrases so formed. Once stated, the philosophy of facts flourished mightily, especially in Cambridge. (21)

It seems to me that Geach is being unfair to facts, and not merely because he likens them to a social disease. That facts are in *general* attributable to that-clauses would be hard to maintain after reading Austin. Geach, of course, is only trying to account for the contagion among philosophers. Even so, there is reason to doubt his etiology. The nineteenth-century philosophers surveyed all used the word "fact" either in ways that were current *before* the advent of the phrase "fact that" or in ways that do not really go together with it, e.g., senses (5) and (6). One of them, Mill, wrote well before the turn of the century, and, as we shall see in the next chapter, there is circumstantial evidence tying Peirce's use to his. Bradley might have preferred not to acknowledge the influence of the despised Mill, but he knew his enemy well. In any case, ideas are not bacilli, and Geach does not explain why philosophers felt a need for the notion of a fact at this time.

Preoccupation with the phrase "fact that" might lead us to suppose that the answer has to do with the correspondence theory of truth: facts are needed to give sentences something to correspond to. For a number of reasons, I do not think that this explanation is satisfactory. In the first place, Bradley and Peirce were hardly advocates of the correspondence theory. On the contrary, they are commonly, if somewhat misleadingly, regarded as point men for its chief competitors, the coherence theory and pragmatism. Secondly, the correspondence theory has a long history, going back to Plato, or at least Aristotle. During practically the entire period, correspondence was held to be to things, not facts. The statement that this paper is white was supposedly true in virtue of its correspondence to the paper itself rather than to any fact. Hence, bringing in correspondence does nothing to solve the problem, because we still have to explain why correspondence to things gave way to correspondence to facts.

Hacking thinks that he has an answer to this question. It has to do with what he calls "the problem of articulation," i.e., "how articulated language effects the representation of a non-articulated part of the world." (87) The sentence "this paper is white" is articulated: it has a subject and a predicate. The paper itself, on the other hand, is non-articulated:

its whiteness is not something separate from it. Thus both subject and predicate seem to refer to the same white paper, but to do so in different ways, and the question is how. Hacking thinks that Wittgenstein, at any rate, introduced facts in order to solve this problem. For the fact that this paper is white consists of the paper and the property of whiteness, and is thus articulated in the very same way as the sentence is.

If anyone was ever worried about the problem of articulation, I suppose Wittgenstein was, since he held that propositions are *pictures* of facts. But I doubt very much that he introduced facts in order to solve it. For the problem will clearly arise *whenever* a sentence is more finely articulated than the object to which it allegedly corresponds, and not just in the limiting case in which the former is articulated and the latter not. But according to Wittgenstein, this happens all the time. One of the most frequently discussed passages in the *Tractatus* is 3.1432, which states that "instead of, 'The complex sign "*aRb*" says that *a* stands to *b* in the relation *R*,' we ought to put, '*That* "*a*" stands to "*b*" in a certain relation says *that aRb.*'" As usually, and I think correctly, interpreted, this means that the fact that *aRb* has as constituents only *a* and *b*, not *a*, *b*, and *R*. In order to get the *proposition* that *aRb* to picture this fact, Wittgenstein has to treat it too as having only two constituents, unlike the sentence, which has three. If facts were introduced to solve the problem of articulation, they are obviously a failure. I consider it far more likely that Wittgenstein came to language with his metaphysics of facts already in place.

It is no accident that facts come on the scene at a time when relations begin to be taken seriously. I said above that Mill used facts in connection with relations, and we shall see just how in the next chapter. Bradley, who was obsessed with relations, argued, as we shall see in Chapter 3, that they are intelligible only in terms of facts. We have already seen how Peirce, who next to Russell was the philosopher most responsible for making relations respectable, replaced Aristotle's category of substance with that of fact in order to accommodate them. Russell himself can hardly be accused of underestimating their importance:

> The question of relations is one of the most important that arise in philosophy, as most other issues turn on it: monism and pluralism; the question whether anything is wholly true except the whole of truth, or wholly real except the whole of reality; idealism and realism, in some of their forms; perhaps the very existence of philosophy as a subject distinct from science and possessing a method of its own. (1971, 333)

As he sees it, traditional metaphysics did violence to relations by trying to reduce them to properties. On what he calls the "monadistic" theory, they are properties of the individuals standing in the relation. As Russell observes, this was Leibniz's approach. But as we shall see in the next chapter, it was really the standard view up until the nineteenth century. On what he calls the "monistic" theory, they are properties rather of the whole composed of the individuals in question. He attributes this view to Bradley, with what justice we shall see in Chapter 3. Both theories come to grief on asymmetrical relations, according to Russell (1956, 221–6).[13] It is because of relations that the world cannot be completely described "by a lot of particulars," as Russell put it. In addition to the cup and the saucer we must take account of the cup's being on the saucer, which is a fact. As long as relations could be swept under the rug of properties, the need for facts did not arise. For a thing's properties were pictured as inhering in it, so that given the totality of things the world was completely determined.

[13] In the case of the monadistic theory, for example, a's being greater than b cannot merely consist in a's having a certain magnitude M and b's having another magnitude m, since it would also have to be the case that M is greater than m, and the attempt to reduce this relation to properties of M and m would lead to a vicious regress. On the monistic theory, a's being greater than b consists in the possession of a property by the whole (ab). But this is the same as the whole (ba). Hence a's being greater than b is the same as b's being greater than a.

Chapter 2

Relations and Their Foundations

The House that Aristotle Built

The picture of reality as consisting of a number of mutually independent things, each having various properties and persisting amid change, so commends itself to common sense as to render superfluous any further explanation for the long sway held by the notions of substance and attribute over Western philosophy. Nonetheless, such explanations have been forthcoming. Russell saw substances and attributes as epiphenomena of subjects and predicates. No one, he said, whose language lacked the latter would ever have come up with the former. (1971, 330) Peirce had quite a different explanation: it is not that metaphysics imitated common sense but just the opposite. "Ordinary men," he said, "live so completely within the house of the Stagyrite that whatever they see out of the windows appears to them incomprehensible and metaphysical." (1, vii)

The basic structure of this house was erected already in the *Categories.* There it is laid down that only individual things, e.g., particular men and horses, are capable of independent existence. These are the primary substances. (2^a34) The species and genera to which these individuals belong—natural kinds like man and animal—are called secondary substances. Primary and secondary substances together make up the category of substance. (2^a11) The remaining categories—quantity, quality, relation, action, passion, place, time, position, and state—comprise attributes of substances, individual attributes as well as the species and genera to which they belong; color and shape, for example, being *species* of quality, not individual qualities. On one interpretation, individual attributes are universals, such as whiteness. On another, they are particulars, such as the whiteness of this piece of paper, considered as distinct from the whiteness of another, exactly similar, piece of paper. Things in non-substance categories are said to exist *in* substances. The second interpretation seems to make better sense of this, as well as of the statement that secondary substances are not in primary substances but are *said of* them. (2^a34) Ockham took this as showing that Aristotle was talking about words instead of things, but this does not seem to be the case. (1974, 133) In any case, however, he made a distinction between the relation in which a primary substance stands to its attributes and that in which it stands to the species and genera to which it belongs. If the individuals of non-substance categories are particulars, then, for example, a white man can be said to contain an instance of whiteness, but to be himself an instance of humanity. Neither attributes nor secondary substances, however, can exist apart from primary substances. (2^a34) Finally, primary substances are distinguished by the fact that they can "receive contraries," i.e., persist through change. One and the same man can be pale at one time and dark at another. Aristotle goes so far as to say that this is what is "most distinctive of substance." (4^a10)

Aristotle does not speak of species and genera as secondary substances in his other works and subsequent philosophers use the word "substance" for whatever has the characteristics ascribed to *primary* substances in the *Categories*. That is, substances (1) are individual things, (2) have attributes, (3) can exist independently, and (4) can persist through change.[1] Aristotle himself seems later to have changed his mind about what primarily deserves the name "substance," since in Metaphysics Z he identifies it with the essence. Since the latter is not peculiar to the individual, but is rather common to all the members of a species, this is hard to reconcile with (1).[2]

Russell has taught us to regard relations as holding *between* things. But the above scheme has no room for relations so conceived. Since relations are not themselves substances, they can only be attributes inhering in substances. Aristotle himself had no noun for "relation." Instead he used the prepositional phrase *προς τι*, which literally means "towards something."

---

1 A similar list is given by Bergmann (160), except that he speaks of "natures," i.e., complete sets of properties, instead of attributes. O'Connor, writing in the *Encyclopedia of Philosophy* (s.v. "Substance and Attribute") lists all the features mentioned above together with those of being "a logical subject" and "a core of essential properties." But he is concerned to list all the ways in which Aristotle defines "substance" in his writngs, which he admits to be probably inconsistent, whereas I am content for the time being to stick to the account given in the *Categories*.

2 Most of the Scholastics tried to do so by denying that humanity in Plato, say, is literally the same as humanity in Socrates. If it is the same, then Plato and Socrates cannot be identical with their essences without being the same as each other.

Moreover, in the *Categories* he never defines relations directly but contents himself with a definition of "relatives" ($\tau\alpha$ $\pi\rho o s$ $\tau\iota$), by which he means the actual things standing in a relation: "We call *relatives* all such things as are said to be just what they are, *of* or *than* other things, or in some other way, *in relation to* something else." ($6^a 36$) In the *Metaphysics*, however, he goes on to define the relations themselves: 'Further there are the properties in virtue of which the things which possess them are called relative; e.g., "equality" is relative because "the equal" is relative, and "similarity" because "the similar" is relative.' ($1021^b 6$–8)

But notice that the relations so defined are not the now familiar "Russellian" relations that hold *between* things. They are rather properties *belonging* to things: in modern parlance, relational properties. We can distinguish two classes of relational properties. The one includes such properties as being a brother of Hector, which involve particulars. The other includes such properties as being a brother, which do not. The latter are nevertheless relational, since a brother must be a brother of someone. Given Russellian relations and modern quantification theory we can say how the two classes are related. The first contains properties of the form $x[xRa]$ and the second those of the form $x[(\exists y)xRy]$.[3] It is a weakness of the Aristotelian view of relations that it cannot give any such account. In the above quotation from the *Metaphysics*, the expressions "the equal" and "the similar" must, if *complete*, refer to relational properties of the second class. But it is more likely that these expressions are elliptical and signify relations to definite but unspecified individuals. Such suppression of the second term of a relation, which is frequent in the Aristotelian tradition, makes it all the easier to suppose that we are dealing with a property of a thing rather than a relation between things.

Relations in God

Relations acquire an enhanced significance in the Middle Ages, for reasons that seem initially to have more to do with theology than with philosophy. The problem was how to understand the doctrine of the Trinity. To what do the names "Father," "Son," and "Holy Spirit" refer? They cannot refer to the divine nature as such, because in that case they would all refer to the same thing, which would contradict the fact that the three persons are distinct. The answer given by St. Augustine, following the lead of certain

[3] I use "$x[\ldots x \ldots]$" to indicate property abstraction. For example, $x[x \text{ is red}]$ is the property of being red.

Greek fathers, was that they are *relative* names, implying the existence of relations, i.e., relational properties, in God.[4]

This solution was eventually endorsed by ecclesiastical councils. But it created new problems of its own.[5] For it was generally assumed that predication in non-substance categories was always accidental rather than essential. The picture was of properties *inhering* in the substance like pins in a pincushion, which can always be removed and replaced with other pins. At least, this was true of created things. But nothing in God could be accidental, since that would make him subject to change, contradicting his immutability. In any case, the doctrine of the Trinity was not regarded as contingently true, as it would be if the divine relations were mere accidents. Augustine's solution was simply to deny that what is true of created things is necessarily true of God. Relations are not accidents in God, as they are in creatures. But he did not say whether their relation to the divine nature is inherence or identity, these being the only recognized alternatives.

A related problem had already arisen in the *Categories* with regard to the differentiating properties of species. It would seem, for example, that rationality, which is the differentia of the species man, cannot simply inhere in men as an attribute, as do the members of non-substance categories. Its relation to substance must be more intimate than that. On the other hand, it is not itself a species or genus, and would thus seem to be disqualified from standing in the "said of" relation, the only other possibility permitted by the *Categories*. Be that as it may, Aristotle says, with apparent inconsistency, that such properties *are* said of substance, no doubt because of this very dilemma (3^a21).[6]

The *Categories*, in the Latin translation of Boethius, had an enormous influence in the Middle Ages, partly because for a long time it was one of very few works of Aristotle's available in the West. In this translation *προς τι* is rendered both by its literal equivalent *ad aliquid* and by the substantive *relativum.*[7] Both these expressions refer to the things standing in a relation. But Latin, unlike Greek, also has a word, *relatio*, for the relation itself, and it is from this that the category takes its traditional name. Relations, however, continue to be thought of as properties *belonging*

---

[4] Thus in *The Trinity* Augustine writes that the difference between being the Father and being the Son does not imply a difference of substance because these terms are in the category of relation rather than substance (5.5.6).

[5] For further details, see vol. 6 of the Blackfriars edition of Acquinas' *Summa Theologiae*, app. 6, "Divine Relations."

[6] See Ackrill's note in his translation (85).

[7] See the Greek-Latin glossary appended to the Latin text (Aristotle 1961), s.v. *προς τι*, which also lists the individual occurrences.

to things rather than as something holding between them.[8] Sometimes they are described in terms of an internal tendency of one thing towards another.

In the *Summa Theologiae* (1a.28.2), Aquinas states that each of the "nine categories of accidental being," i.e., the non-substance categories, has two aspects. On the one hand, since each such category is made up of attributes inhering in things, there is what he calls its *inesse*, or existence in a subject. On the other hand, there is the specific character of the category, which distinguishes it from other categories. In the case of relation, this consists in its reference to another thing, or *ad aliquid.* According to Aquinas, the relations constituting the persons of the Trinity have only the second aspect, not the first.

If the divine relations are not accidents inhering in the divine nature, what is their status? Aquinas held that they are identical with the divine nature itself. But this creates an obvious problem:

> It seems that the relations which are in God are not distinct in reality from each other. Because all things identical with one and the same thing are identical with one another. But every relation in God is identical in reality with the divine nature. Therefore divine relations are not distinct from each other in reality. (1a.28.3)

This is a serious problem because relations were invoked in the first place in order to keep the distinctions between persons from collapsing. Aquinas attempts to solve it by appealing to Aristotle, according to whom, as he states it,

> this argument, that all things identical with one and the same thing are identical with one another, holds good wherever there is identity both in reality and meaning, as, when the same thing is called a 'tunic' and a 'garment', but not where there is a difference of meaning.

The passage to which Aquinas refers occurs in the *Physics* (202^b10). There Aristotle defines movement or change as the actualization of a potentiality. The question arises: where is movement, in the mover or in the moved? If this seems a strange question to ask, perhaps that is because we are accustomed to regard the movement of one thing by another as a relation between them rather than as something that is *in* either of them. But for Aristotle, since movement is not itself a substance it must be in a substance. At first it may seem as if there will always be two movements,

---

[8] Beckman (1967) quotes Scotus as saying that a relation is sometimes regarded as a kind of "interval" or "medium" between things, but Scotus does not in the end endorse this view.

one in the mover and the other in the moved. For each has a potentiality actualized, a potential activity in the one case, and a potential passivity in the other. But Aristotle insists, somewhat surprisingly perhaps, that one and the same movement is the actualization of both of these potentialities and that this movement is in the thing moved, not the mover (202^a15). Otherwise every mover would itself have to be in motion, something that Aristotle denies in the case of the prime mover. But now it appears as if moving and being moved must be the same, since both are identical with one and the same affection in the thing moved. Aristotle denies this on the ground that moving and being moved differ conceptually, or with regard to their *λογος* (202^b21). One is the motion regarded as the actualization of the mover's active potentiality; the other is the same motion regarded as the actualization of the passive potentiality of the thing moved. Aristotle compares them with the road from Thebes to Athens, which from another point of view is the road from Athens to Thebes. The discussion is reminiscent of the opening portion of Frege's "On Sense and Reference," though, according to Frege, so long as we are clear about whether we are talking about senses or references we do not have to restrict the principle of transitivity of identity.

The Latin translation of *λογος* is *ratio*, which is rendered as "meaning" in the quotation from Aquinas. It is frequently translated as "concept." For example, a *distinctio rationis*, or conceptual distinction, is one created by the mind, as opposed to a *distinctio realis*, or real distinction between things. Thus the distinction between the road from Thebes to Athens and the road from Athens to Thebes would be a conceptual one. On the view here attributed to Aristotle, the same would appear to be true of the distinction between moving and being moved. At least this seems to have been the opinion of Aquinas, who in his commentary on the *Physics*, defends against various objections the view—which he ascribes to Aristotle—that "action and passion are one motion and differ only according to reason [*ratio*]." (3:321) In the passage from the *Summa Theologiae* cited above he goes on to apply what he has said about moving and being moved to the problem of relations in God:

> Although changing and change as well as being changed are the same thing, nevertheless it does not follow that changing and being changed are identical; for changing implies the relationship of causing change in another, whereas being changed implies the relationship of being changed by another. Likewise, while both fatherhood and sonship are in reality the same thing as the divine nature, nevertheless their proper meanings imply opposite relationships. (1a.28.3)

This may make it seem as if the divine relations are merely conceptually distinct, but Aquinas does not see it that way. His position rather prefigures Geach's theory of relative identity, according to which two things may be the same F, but not the same G, where F and G are different concepts under which the things fall.[9] In the present case, fatherhood and sonship are the same thing, in virtue of their identity with the divine nature, but not the same relation. At least this is one way of making sense of Aquinas' claim that the relations derive their reality from their identity with the divine nature and their distinctness from each other from the mutual opposition implied by their concepts (*rationes*).

Scotus objected to Aquinas' divergent accounts of the reality of the divine relations, on the one hand, and their distinctness, on the other. He held that we can legitimately speak of "things" (*res*) in such a way that anything that exists outside the mind counts as a thing, no matter what category it may be assigned to. (3.10) This being so, we can always ask whether A is the same or a different thing from B, and this question will always have a determinate answer. In the case of relations, "what accounts for a relation's being a thing that is actual, not just virtual or *in causa*, therefore is also the immediate basis for its being distinct from any relation that is not it." (3.23) If fatherhood and sonship are the same thing as the divine nature, then they are the same thing as each other. There can be at most a conceptual distinction between them, in the sense that, though they apply to the same thing, they represent different ways of conceiving of it. This means in turn that the persons of the Trinity, which are constituted by these relations, differ only conceptually, which is unacceptable from an orthodox point of view.

Scotus' own solution depends on his notion of a formal distinction. Things are *really* distinct from one another provided that they can be separated, even if only by God. Otherwise they are *really* identical. Nonetheless, within one and the same real thing it is possible to distinguish a number of what Scotus calls "formalities" or "realities." (The word "reality," or rather *realitas*, was apparently coined by Scotus.) These are objective components of the thing. They are not created by the mind. At the same time, they cannot be separated even by divine power. For example, sensitivity and rationality are inseparable from the human soul, according to Scotus and other scholastic philosophers. It would be impossible to take away either without destroying the soul itself. Yet sensitivity and rationality are distinct capacities. They are even exemplified separately by the lower animals and angels, respectively. In Scotus' opinion, it is not always good enough to say that we just apply different concepts to

[9] Anscombe and Geach interpret Aquinas in this way (118).

one and the same thing. We must posit an objective basis for certain of these concepts in the thing itself. It is this objective basis for a conceptual distinction that Scotus refers to as a formality. And a distinction having an objective basis of this kind is called a formal distinction. The formal distinction is thus intermediate between a merely conceptual distinction and a real one, in the above sense of "real."[10] Perhaps the most important purely philosophical example of a formal distinction is that between the individuality (*haecceitas*) of a thing and its species or common nature. Socrates' individuality and his humanity are really identical but formally distinct, according to Scotus. But it was in connection with the Trinity that he found the notion most useful. On his view, each of the relations in God is really identical with the divine nature but formally distinct from it. In other words, instead of relativizing identity, as Aquinas appears to, he recognizes two different grades of it, of which formal identity is the stronger, and thus closer to what we mean by identity.

Relations in God are thus exceptions to the characterization of relations as attributes inhering in substances. But this is because their relation to the divine nature is even more intimate than inherance. This means that the divine relations do not belong to the category of relation, since it and the other non-substance categories were regarded as comprising attributes—indeed accidents—of things. But this is not surprising since nothing predicable of both God and creatures was held to fall under any of the categories. Such notions were called transcendental, because they transcend the ten categories. (Wolter, 8–10) Examples are being, one, good. Thus the relations in God are transcendental relations as opposed to those of the category of relation, which were called predicamental relations (after *praedicamentum*, the Latin word for category). But these are not the only examples of transcendental relations. Any relation that is essential to the thing that has it must also be transcendental. For example, the Scholastics held that every creature has an essential relation to God. Many, including Aquinas and Scotus, also held that the human soul has an essential relation to the body. Since these relations are not accidents, they cannot belong to the category of relation. On the contrary, they were held to be one with the substance itself, just as the divine relations are identical with the divine nature.[11] This, as we shall see, is one sense in which nineteenth-century philosophers used the term "internal relation."

---

[10] See Wolter (21–24) and the glossary appended by Alluntis and Wolter to Scotus' *God and Creatures*, s.v. "formal distinction."

[11] See Holzer (33ff) and Horvath (ch. 3).

Fundamentum Relationis

It was a pervasive doctrine in the Middle Ages that every relation involves three things. The first is the thing in which it inheres or is otherwise contained; this is the *subject* of the relation. The second is the thing *to* which it is a relation; this is the *term.* The third is sometimes described as that *in virtue* of which the subject is related to the term; this is the *foundation* of the relation (*fundamentum relationis*).[12]

What sort of thing can serve as the foundation of a relation? Why was a foundation deemed necessary? How is the phrase "in virtue of" to be understood? I shall try to answer each of these questions in turn.

In regard to the first, the philosophers with whom we are presently concerned lived very much within the house of Aristotle. To ask what sort of thing can serve as a foundation is to ask what category or categories foundations are to be found in. The answer seems to be that items of any category, including the category of relation itself, can "found" a relation, but that the process of tracing relations back to their foundations must ultimately terminate in things that are not relative but absolute.[13] This requires some explanation. In the Middle Ages the Aristotelian categories were divided into absolute and relative categories. The latter comprised not only the category of relation itself, but all the categories except substance, quality, and quantity. Only the items in these three categories were thought to involve no reference to anything external to their subjects. The notion of a foundation seems to have been employed at first only in connection with relations proper and to have spread later to the other relative categories. It is perhaps most easily conveyed by way of an example. If I say that this page is the same color as the preceding one, I am asserting a relation whose subject is this page and whose term is the preceding one. The foundation of this relation is a certain quality, the whiteness of this page.

As to why a foundation was deemed necessary, the answer lies in the ambiguous status accorded to relations in the Aristotelian tradition. On the one hand, the relation is supposed to be a kind of internal modification of its subject. On the other hand, it may be acquired or lost for reasons that do not seem to touch the subject itself but depend entirely on the vicissitudes of another thing. Thus Aristotle says in the *Metaphysics* that "the relative is of all the categories in the least degree a definite entity or

---

12 On this and related points, I have benefitted from two telephone conversations with Professor John Boler in Spring 1984.

13 See Scotus (13.16) and Wolter (156). Sometimes the terms "proximate foundation" and "remote foundation" are used in this connection. The subject itself is sometimes regarded as the remote foundation.

substance," giving as reason the alleged fact that "there is no real change in respect of the relative; for without any change in itself one term will be now greater, now smaller or equal, as the other term undergoes quantitative change." (1088^a30) Nevertheless, something is required on the part of the subject too, in this case a certain quantity, and this is the foundation of the relation. Aristotle himself does not use the term "foundation," but certain of his statements seem to have suggested the concept to the Scholastics. Thus Scotus writes:

> It seems that for the Philosopher the foundation for equality is quantity. As he says in the *Categories*: "The most distinctive mark of quantity is that equal and unequal can be predicated with reference to it." The words "with reference to it" indicate the foundation of this relation, just as they do in the chapter on quality: "What is distinctive is this, that we predicate likeness and unlikeness with reference to quality only." These statements about the basis for equality or similarity are further explained, it seems, in the chapter on relation in the *Metaphysics*: "The equal, the similar, and the identical are all predicated with reference to unity. Those things are equal whose quantity is one, those are similar whose quality is one, and those things are identical whose substance is one." Here he seems to suggest that the foundation for equality is not just quantity alone, but a unity of quantity is needed. (6.6)

The last sentence is puzzling. The intended meaning is clearly that the foundation is not just the quantities of the things in question, but the *fact* that they have the *same* quantity. But Scotus' ontology does not have room for such things as facts. Like Aristotle, Scotus held that what is real in the primary sense is the individual substance. Everything else either inheres or is otherwise contained in some individual substance. The *Categories* raised the question of the status of species and genera of the category of substance—what were there called "secondary substances"—and of their relation to individuals of the category. Does the same species, humanity, exist in each human being, or is there a distinct humanity in each? As explained above, it makes better sense of some of Aristotle's statements to interpret individuals of non-substance categories as particulars, which cannot be literally the same in distinct individual substances. But to take the same line with species and genera would seem to defeat their very purpose, which is to account for the fact that distinct individuals can have a common nature. This is presumably one reason why Aristotle says that species and genera are *said of* individual substances, as opposed to being *in* them. The *medieval*, as opposed to the modern, problem of universals was chiefly concerned with the status of species and genera, and not with properties per se. Scotus' solution to it goes a long way towards explaining why he was called the Subtle Doctor. According to him, nothing is *numerically* one in distinct individuals. Nonetheless, a common nature like humanity can be said to be one by what he calls a "less than numerical unity."[14] In other words, just as in the case of identity and diversity, Scotus' strategy is to distinguish different degrees of strength with which a concept can apply. Although he primarily applies the notion of a less than numerical unity to species and genera in the category of substance, it would appear that the unity of quantity mentioned in the last sentence of the above quotation must—if it is anything positive—be of the less than numerical variety, since quantity can no more than anything else be numerically one in distinct individuals. By "a unity of quantity," then, he may mean the *species* in the category of quantity which is less than numerically one in both individuals. For a foundation must be some sort of entity recognized in his ontology, and this is the only one that seems to fit the description. But the *fact* that the quantity is the same in both would fit it better.

Let us now turn to the third question posed above, viz, in what sense the foundation is that "in virtue of" which the subject is related to the term. Aristotle's statements about equality, similarity, and identity leave room for doubt whether he considered these relations to be anything over and above the qualitative and quantitative properties of the things related. And in fact Ockham claimed the authority of Aristotle for his own doctrine of the purely conceptual status of all relations (1974, 158). Scotus, who held that at least some relations exist outside the mind, made a distinction between *intrinsically* and *extrinsically* advenient relations. Whereas an intrinsically advenient relation "is a necessary consequence of its foundation once the terms are given," an extrinsically advenient relation "is not a necessary consequence of the foundation even if the terms are given." (11.34) Intrinsically advenient relations are those of which we are most inclined to suppose that they are nothing over and above their foundations, though Scotus does not invariably draw this conclusion. According to him, the distinction between the category of relation and the other six relative categories consists in the fact that items in the category of relation are all intrinsically advenient relations, whereas those in the last six categories are extrinsically advenient. The sense in which that foundation is that in virtue of which the subject is related to the term will clearly be quite different in the two cases.

As an example of an intrinsically advenient relation, we may take the relation of similarity with regard to color which this page bears to its predecessor. By what was said above, the foundation of this relation ought to

---

[14] For a fuller discussion than I am able to provide here, see Boler (46-50).

be the whiteness of this page. But does the relation really follow necessarily from this foundation once the subject and term are given? Isn't something further required, namely, the whiteness of the preceding page? Or is this supposed to be given along with the term? In that case, why not say that the relation follows necessarily once the subject and term are given, since the foundation is presumably given along with the subject? As a matter of fact, Scotus sometimes saysjust this.[15] This way of talking suggests that the foundation does not represent an *additonal* requisite over and above the subject and the term, but rather something contained in them. Not everything about the subject and term is relevant, however, and so we characterize the relation more precisely when we give the foundation as well. But in cases where the relation was thought to make no difference to the term, e.g., relations of creatures to God, the foundation really was held to exist only in the subject of the relation.

In a passage from the *Metaphysics* that was much discussed in the Middle Ages Aristotle distinguishes three types of relatives:

> Things are called "relative" (a) In the sense that "the double" is relative to the half, and "the triple" to the third; and in general the "many times greater" to the "many times smaller," and that which exceeds to the thing exceeded. (b) In the sense that the thing which heats or cuts is relative to the thing heated or cut; and in general the active to the passive. (c) In the sense that the measurable is relative to the measure, and the knowable to knowledge, and the sensible to sensation. (1020^b26)

The Scholastics construed this classification as based on the foundations of the relations in question. Those of the first type were held to have foundations in the category of quantity, while those of the second type were held to have foundations in the categories of action and passion. But the third type does not seem to consist, as do the first two, of relations having foundations in some common category or categories. (Perhaps for this reason Aquinas, in the *Summa Theologiae* (1a.28.4), attributes to Aristotle the view that every relation is based either on quantity or on action and passion, ignoring the third type altogether.) On what basis, then is the third type distinguished from the other two? According to Scotus, the distinction consists in the fact that relations of the first two types are

---

[15] For example in 13.64: "The relation in this case is said to be in the substance of both terms in the sense that the proximate basis or reason for grounding the relation is in both." "Proximate basis" here translates the Latin *fundamentum proximum* and "reason for grounding" translates *ratio fundandi*. It seems that Scotus is consciously extending the usual notion of foundation. See below.

mutual while those of the third type are non-mutual. A mutual relation is one for which there is a foundation in both the subject and the term, whereas a non-mutual relation has a foundation only in one of the two related things. (13.66) This represents Scotus' interpretation of Aristotle's own explanation, which is that something is called thinkable, say, because there is a thought which thinks it. On Scotus' interpretation, this means that the thought has a real relation to the thing thought, but not vice versa. This in turn is taken to consist in the fact that the foundation for the relation is entirely on the side of the thought. Any plausibility this doctrine may possess no doubt derives in part from the fact that a thing is in some sense unaffected by being thought of. But the real question ought to be whether there is not also something on the side of the thing which makes it and no other the object of the thought.

Since Scotus' distinction between mutual and non-mutual relations makes sense only on the assumption that some relations have a foundation in both the subject and the term there can be no doubt that he accepted this assumption. Why, then, does he sometimes speak as though the notion of a foundation pertains exclusively to the subject? The idea of a foundation is originally that of a necessary condition that the subject must satisfy in order to have the relation in question. In the case of an extrinsically advenient relation this is all it can ever amount to, for the following reason. Take the case of movement discussed above. The mover's property of causing motion in the thing moved belongs to the category of action, which is a category of extrinsically advenient relations according to Scotus. Its foundation is the active *potentiality* of the mover. In like manner, the passive potentiality of the thing moved is the foundation for its property of being moved, which belongs to the category of passion. Being moved is in scholastic terminology the "opposite"—in modern terms the "converse"—of the relation of moving. Given that a has the relation R to b, it follows that b has the opposite relation R' to a. Since the foundation of a relation is a necessary condition on the part of the subject, it follows from the fact that a has the relation R to b that a also has the foundation P of R. Likewise, it follows from b's having R' to a that b has the foundation Q of R'. Hence, if either a has R to b or b has R' to a, it follows both that a has P and b has Q. But the converse is not true. One thing may have the capacity to move another and the second the capacity to be moved by the first without any motion occurring. If we really want to, we can think of Q as the foundation of R in its *term* b and P as the foundation of R' in *its* term a. But nothing is gained by doing so. We can say everything we want to in terms of foundations in the subject and converse relations. Only in the case of intrinsically advenient relations is there any point in speaking of a foundation in the term as well as in the subject. For in the case of such relations, a's having P and b's having Q together constitute a *sufficient* condition for a's having the relation R to b. This is not equivalent to the conjunction of (1) the statement that a's having P is a sufficient condition for a's having the relation R to b and (2) the statement that b's having Q is a sufficient condition for b's having R' to a, since both of these statements are false. Thus we cannot make the point about sufficient conditions if we just assume a foundation in the subject, not even if we bring in converse relations, as we did in the previous case. If we want to be able to make it, we must admit foundations in the term as well.

Are relations anything over and above their foundations? By definition, extrinsically advenient relations are. And since every relation is *in* its subject, even an intrinsically advenient relation must be distinct from its foundation in the *term*. But it must also be distinct from its foundation in the subject, since it can be acquired or lost without any change in the latter. Strictly speaking, this is true only of predicamental relations, since a transcendental relation is essential to its subject. But even a transcendental relation is never *formally* identical with its foundation, according to Scotus, though unlike a predicamental relation it is not really distinct from it, since the two are inseparable even by divine power.

Ockham agreed that relations cannot be identical with their foundations, for the reasons just given. At the same time, he denied that a relation can ever be anything existing outside the mind distinct from absolute things. He had a number of arguments for this conclusion, most of which exploit the ambiguous status of relations in the substance-attribute ontology to which he was committed. As indicated above, the ambiguity consists in the fact that a relation is supposed on the one hand to be contained in its subject and on the other to connect subject and term. Ockham held that the former requirement was incompatible with the latter. In order to connect one thing with another a relation would have to inhere in both, which is impossible in the Aristotelian scheme of things. Hence there could be no such attribute as philosophers supposed a relation to be. Furthermore, if a relation exists in its subject as something distinct from its foundation, then it can also exist without the foundation. Take, for example, the relation of paternity that a father has to his son. The foundation of this relation is the act of generation on the part of the father. Ockham observes that if paternity is indeed something in the father that is distinct from the act of generation, it is in the father after that act is past. But God could have created anything that now exists *in its present state*, without first creating anything that in fact preceded it. Hence God could make a man a father who had never generated offspring. (1974, 163) Yet another absurd consequence of the view in question, according to Ockham, is that every heavenly body would undergo a change in itself whenever a donkey moved from one place to another. For it would lose one spatial relation to the donkey and acquire another. (162)

All of these arguments depend on the conception of relations as contained in their subjects. But Ockham also gives another argument that would seem to apply to relations no matter how conceived. Certain philosophers, including Scotus, had maintained that it is necessary to posit relations existing outside the mind in order to account for the unity of the universe, claiming the authority of Aristotle for this view. Ockham concedes that according to Aristotle the unity of the universe consists in the order of its parts to one another. But by this

> he understands nothing other than that for the universe to be one is for the parts to be so ordered—not that the order or unity is something distinct in reality from every part and all parts of the universe, for so would be to proceed to infinity. For that thing would be ordered to the others, and consequently, by the very same argument, there would be another thing outside of that and the others, which would be their order; and there would be an infinite sequence. Nor does it avail to say that there is a stop at the second step, since with equal ease a stop can be posited at the first; and plurality should never be posited without necessity. (1983, 685)

This of course, is the argument later made famous by Bradley (and vice versa). It is also discussed by Scotus and appears to have originated with Avicenna.[16] It is interesting to see how Ockham moves to head off the standard reply that while relations are needed to connect other things with one another, they do not need anything else to connect them with their terms. The reason usually given is that it is the nature of relations to relate, just it is in the nature of glue to stick to things; we do not need more glue to glue the glue to the things we are gluing together. This reply is what Ockham calls positing a stop at the second step. But if we're going to have to posit such a stop anyway, then why not at the very beginning, before the regress gets started? Why not, in other words, simply say that the things themselves are such as to form a unity? This is just what Ockham does say. The same move was later made by Bradley and Wittgenstein, but with one important difference. They gave ontological status to the unities thus formed, under the name "facts." Ockham's ontology makes it impossible for him to account for the unity he posits. For the things that allegedly form this unity are still individual substances in the Aristotelian mold, whose mutual independence has only been confirmed by Ockham's destructive critique of his predecessors' theories of relations. No matter

[16] See Beckman (78) for Scotus, and Horvath (32) for Avicenna.

that that critique was largely *warranted* by the fact that relations do not fit the Aristotelian scheme. By eliminating them from the world of things, Ockham made that scheme internally consistent at the expense of exposing its inadequacy to plain view.[17]

Ockham's own doctrine is that relations are names. By a name, however, he understood primarily a concept in the mind. He argues at length that this was also the view of Aristotle. Like Aristotle, he pays more attention to relatives than to relations. But according to him a relative is a *name* like "father," not the man to which it applies. (1974, 159) These relative names stand for individuals. The only difference between them and other names standing for individuals is that it is always possible to add to them the name of something else in an oblique case. Thus a father is always a father *of* someone, something similar is always similar *to* something, etc.. Ockham calls terms like "father" and "similar" *concrete* relative terms as opposed to terms like "paternity" and "similarity," which he calls *abstract* relative terms. In like manner, "white" is concrete, "whiteness" abstract. But whereas "whiteness" stands for a quality inhering in the thing to which "white" applies, "paternity" does not stand for anything inhering in the thing to which "father" applies. Although it is a name it is not, strictly speaking, a name *of* anything. Abstract relative names are thus used improperly where they purport to refer to relations inhering in things. But sometimes, Ockham thinks, they serve as kind of shorthand for more explicit forms of expression in which only individuals are mentioned. Examples are "the father is a father by paternity" and "the similar is similar by similarity," which on analysis become "the father is a father because he begot a son" and "the similar is similar because it has a quality of the same sort as something else." (163) Thus abstract relatives, where they are legitimate at all, are dispensable according Ockham.

Concrete relatives are another story. On the one hand, Ockham asserts that nothing exists except absolute things, under which he includes only substances and their accidents in the category of quality. On the other hand, he does not go so far as to maintain that a complete account of the world can dispense entirely with relative terms. His doctrine seems to be rather that there are true propositions which are irreducibly relational, but what makes any such proposition true is one or more absolute things. One is tempted to say, using Scotus' terminology, that according to Ockham every relation is intrinsically advenient. For every relation is for him a necessary

[17] Whitehead remarks (208) that although there is really no room for relations in a substance-attribute metaphysics this fact was not noticed at first because Aristotle was inconsistent in this regard. He credits Descartes with the first *consistent* substance-attribute metaphysics.

consequence of its foundation, in the sense that given the relevant absolutes the truth or falsity of every relational propostion is already determined. But the term "advenient" is really out of place here because it implies that the relation is something that accrues to the thing over and above the foundation. According to Ockham, there is no such thing, but only the relative *term*, which is a concept existing in the mind.

We thus have relative concepts but only absolute things. Why does a given relative term apply to one thing and fail to apply to another? Ockham seems to have no answer to this question. To say that a man is a father because he begot a son is only to elucidate one relational proposition by means of another, not to explain what makes relational propositions true. And Ockham is fully aware of this. The point of the example was to show how to dispense with abstract relatives, not to give an analysis of relational propositions. The conclusion that Ockham drew from the regress argument is that no analysis can be given. Things are ordered, that is, there are true relational propositions. But the order obtaining among things is not something distinct from things themselves, that is, there are no relations existing outside the mind.

Ockham's theory of relations is nominalistic. This will come as no surprise to those who are accustomed to regarding Ockham as a nominalist. But it is worth noting that his nominalism with regard to relations is in addition to his position on universals and is not implied by it. The issue of nominalism versus realism can arise with regard to a broad range of subjects. Historically speaking, it first arose in connection with universals, i.e., species and genera chiefly in the category of substance, though the same considerations apply to species and genera of other categories as well. The realist insisted that it is necessary to posit "common natures" in the things themselves in order to explain why the concepts apply to them. A characteristic response on the part of the nominalist is to deny that any explanation is required. The proposition that Morris is a cat is true simply in virtue of Morris himself, not because of any feline nature he shares with others of his kind. (With regard to *individuals*, such as Morris, the Scholastics were all realists. But what if we extend the nominalist treatment to them as well? Then what makes our proposition true? Reality as a whole perhaps? Or do we deny that any explanation is necessary?) To see that Ockham's nominalism with regard to relations is not part and parcel of his position on universals it suffices to consider his views on qualities. These he held to be things existing outside the mind, distinct from the substances in which they inhere. Since Ockham rejected Scotus' formal distinction, he took this to mean that qualities can exist in *separation* from substance, though only by divine power. Thus the whiteness of this page is as much a real thing as the page itself. It is not, however, the same thing as the whiteness of the preceding page, nor is there anything common to the two whitenesses in virtue of which one and the same concept applies to both. In other words, Ockham is a realist with regard to qualities and a nominalist with regard to universals. This is possible only because individuals in the category of quality were not regarded as universals. But Ockham's arguments against the reality of relations do not depend on the assumption that relations are universals. On the contrary, with the exception of the regress argument, they all depend on the assumption that a relation is contained in its subject, a condition which the medieval mind found hard to reconcile with universality, as attested by Scotus' doctrine of the less than numerical unity, mentioned above. The arguments in question all go to show what a Procrustes' bed the Aristotelian scheme was when it came to relations. But Ockham's own theory is hardly any more satisfactory, since it makes a complete mystery of relational propositions.

We shall have more to say about the regress argument in the next chapter. Unlike the other arguments, it is directed not so much against the possibility of real relations as against their utility. For the main task such relations were supposed to perform is that of unifying the manifold. The regress argument purports to show that they are unfitted for this task. But Ockham has nothing to take their place. For according to him the world is made up of a plurality of mutually independent things. These things can be brought together in true propositions. But what makes such propositions true is not a *real* unity corresponding to the mental unity that is the proposition, but rather the separate things themselves. We saw above that you can have nominalism with regard to all sorts of things. This is nominalism with regard to unity, which, as we shall see, is not at all the same thing as nominalism with regard to relations.

Facts as Foundations

John Locke's account of relations in the *Essay* employs much of the scholastic conceptual framework and terminology explored above. In spirit, at least, it is nominalistic. There is no talk of relations as such, but only of relative terms, which are characterized as terms that cannot be applied to one thing without at the same time "intimating" some other thing, e.g., a father is necessarily the father *of* someone. The novelty of Locke's account is contained in his remarks about the foundation of a relation, which is initially described in psychological terms as "the occasion why the mind thus brings two things together and, as it were, takes a view of them at once." (1:266) This may give the impression that it is all a matter of subjective association. There is no telling what might conceivably make a given mind have a given thought. But the question why the mind brings together a given pair of things may require, not so much a causal explanation of its act of judging, as a *justification* of the resulting judgement. And Locke's examples show that when he identifies the foundation with an "occasion why the mind brings two things together," what he has in mind is a fact or event actually involving the two things and justifying the application of the relative term to one of them. Thus the foundation for applying the term "husband" to Caius is "the contract and ceremony of marriage with Sempronia," while the relation of hen and chick has a foundation that consists in one's having laid the egg out of which the other was hatched. Locke does not stop to inquire what sort of entity this might be. If he had, he might have discovered that he had avoided positing relations only by introducing a new category of *facts*. In a sense, this is what was wanted all along. For example, when Scotus said that the foundation of equality is not simply quantity but a unity of quantity, what he was struggling to say—and what the Aristotelian framework prevented his saying—is that it is really the fact that two things have the same quantity that makes them equal. Equality is a prime example of what Scotus calls an intrinsically advenient relation. If any relations are reducible to non-relational properties of their terms, these are. But since the quantity of one thing is not numerically identical with that of any other, sameness of quantity is a relation between really distinct entities, and any attempt to reduce it in turn to non-relational properties of the quantities themselves would generate a vicious regress. This is presumably why Scotus denied that quantity is a sufficient foundation for equality and required instead a unity of quantity. In the case of so-called extrinsically advenient relations, on the other hand, there was never any question of a reduction to non-relational properties. Ockham sought to reduce these along with all other relations to relative names, but he was left without any account of what it is about a thing that makes such a term apply. Locke supplies this deficiency by referring us to a fact about the thing that warrants our applying the term in question. But he does not seem to be aware that this account commits him to the existence of facts as entites in their own right. There is certainly no provision for such entities in the subject-attribute metaphysics that he inherited and never renounced.

Locke's remarks may, however, have influenced another Englishman, one who had less reverence for the categories of Aristotle. At any rate, John Stuart Mill tells us in his *Autobiography* (47) that he not only read Locke's *Essay*, in his youth but prepared a detailed abstract and commentary on each chapter to serve as a text for discussions of that work with his father. He adds that this took place at the time when his father was beginning his *Analysis of the Phenomena of the Human Mind*, a fact whose relevance will emerge shortly. As far as the Aristotelian categories are concerned, after listing them in his *System of Logic*, he blandly remarks that "the imperfections of this classification are too obvious to require, and its merits are not sufficient to reward, a minute examination." (29) He compares it to "a division of animals into men, quadrupeds, horses, asses, and ponies" and mentions as one of its chief deficiencies the fact that it takes account of nothing except substances and attributes (30). In the same work, he offers what he considers to be a clear and simple explanation of relations and relative names, "a subject so long the opprobrium of metaphysics." He does not take credit for this explanation himself, but says that it was first given by his father in his *Analysis of the Phenomena of the Human Mind.* But a comparison of the two accounts suggests that there is more of filial piety than of truth in this statement.

According to the elder Mill, the chief peculiarity of relative terms is that they always come in pairs. As examples he gives: father and son; husband and wife; master and servant; subject and king; high and low; right and left; antecedent and consequent. (2:6) Such terms are called *correlative.* The paired terms do not have to be different, however, since some words are capable of serving as their own correlatives, e.g. brother, sister, cousin, friend, like, equal, etc. We give such names to things because they habitually present themselves in pairs, or are "joined by association," to use the psychological jargon favored by Mill. Of course, not all things so joined have correlative names attached to them, but only those for which such names prove useful because of their frequent occurrence or their importance to us.

So far, James Mill's account is essentially the same as Locke's, in which a relative term is one that intimates something in addition to what it stands for. The only difference is that it is stated entirely in terms of names as opposed to the things those names stand for. In this respect it resembles Ockham's definition of a relative term as one to which another term can always be applied in an oblique case. (The Latin grammarian Priscian, in a passage cited by Ockham (1974, 161), provides a somewhat closer parallel, emphasizing like Mill the existence of correlatives.) But Locke, too, mentioned the phenomenon of correlative terms, observing that we are more likely to be aware of relations for which such pairs of terms exist. But he also pointed out that not every relative term has a correlative term associated with it. For example, " concubine" is no less a relative term than "wife," though it lacks a correlative (267). Mill says that every relative term has a correlative "either actual or implied." (6) Presumably this means that a relative term implies the existence of something in addition to what it stands for, even if there is no established term for it. But this is just Locke's position. Unlike Locke, however, Mill does not explain how these terms function.

Although John Stuart Mill claims only to be reporting his father's account, what he actually provides is a theory of his own having some affinity with Locke's. Relative terms are a species of "concrete generals," in the vocabulary he took over from the Scholastics. A general term denotes an indefinite number of objects, unlike a singular term, which denotes only one. Thus "husband" is general because it denotes every married man. It is concrete because it denotes things as opposed to attributes; terms denoting the latter are called "abstract." It is characteristic of concrete general terms to have connotation as well as denotation. In the case of most such terms the connotation will be an *attribute* possessed by every object falling within the denotation. Thus the concrete general term "white" *denotes* every white thing and *connotes* the attribute whiteness. In contrast, a proper name like "John" has only denotation; it gives no information about its object.

What is the connotation of a relative term? We might perhaps expect it to be a relation or relational property. But Mill seems to think that this would be projecting onto the world a plurality that exists only in language. According to him,

> if we take any two correlative names, father and son, for instance, though the objects denoted by the names are different, they both, in a certain sense, connote the same thing. They cannot, indeed, be said to connote the same attribute; to be a father is not the same thing as to be a son. But when we call one man a father, another a son, what we mean to affirm is a set of facts, which are exactly the same in both cases. To predicate of *A* that he is the father of *B*, and of *B* that he is the son of *A*, is to assert one and the same fact in different words. (1956, 27)

This fact, says Mill, can be analyzed into "a series of physical events or phenomena, in which both *A* and *B* are parties concerned." Whether he thinks that this is true of facts in general he does not say. As we shall see presently, he gives as examples some facts that do not appear to be so analyzable.

In a case such as the above, Mill says that the fact "constitutes" the relation. He attributes this doctrine to the Scholastics, who allegedly called such a fact the "foundation" of the relation for just this reason (28). But he does not say which of the "schoolmen" is supposed to have taught this doctrine. In his *Autobiography* he mentions having read "the whole or parts of the Latin treatises on the scholastic logic" (20), but neither there nor in the *System of Logic*, where he often avails himself of scholastic vocabulary, does he mention individual scholastic philosophers by name. There are, however, general grounds for doubting that any medieval philosopher took the position described by Mill. For them, the foundation of a relation was something *contained* in a substance, not something in which two or more substances can take part. There was no room for facts *chez Aristote.* Mill's interpretation may have been based on a misunderstanding of certain statements about relations whose foundations are themselves relative. For example, paternity was held to be founded in the father's act of generating a son. Mill takes this as a fact or a series of events. But the scholastics treated it instead as a property of the father, belonging to the category of action. (This is a relative, as opposed to an absolute, category, which means that it consists of relational properties. All relatives were held to be founded ultimately in absolutes. But except in the category of relation itself—which Scotus, at least, understood as comprising only intrinsically advenient relations—the foundation was not regarded as a sufficient condition for the relation. Thus the act of generation was founded in turn in the father's generative capacity, but in no sense reducible to it.)

But Mill is concerned less with the correct interpretation of scholastic doctrine than with the correct theory of relations. And his theory of facts as foundations is motivated not by deference to authority, but by an intuition which we shall see shared by thinkers of the most diverse temperaments in the century following the publication of the *System of Logic.* This is the view that—contrary to what language would lead us to believe—the sort of thing expressed by a whole sentence is metaphysically more basic than some of the things expressed by the words making it up. Thus Mill regards facts and individuals as real but gives a nominalistic analysis of attributes and relations. Any fact or series of facts involving two things can be taken, he says, as constituting a relational property of either (1956, 43). He adds that any two things are involved in some such fact, since it is common to all things to be "members of the universe." So enamored was he with the idea of a foundation that he saw in it the key to all attributes, which he assimilated to relational properties with a suppressed mental term. Thus he says that the whiteness of snow is "grounded on its exciting in us the sensation of white," and calls this the foundation of the quality. (42)

Some of Mill's statements suggest that he thinks of facts as physical entities like events. This would explain why he did not find it necessary to argue explicitly for their existence, and also why he considered them less problematic entities than relations and attributes. But this interpretation does not sit well with all of his examples, some of which are of a more abstract nature:

> Thus in the relation of greater and less between to magnitudes, the *fundamentum relationis* is the fact that one of the two magnitudes could, under certain conditions, be included in, without entirely

> filling, the space occupied by the other magnitude. In the relation of master and servant, the *fundamentum relationis* is the fact that one has undertaken, or is compelled, to perform certain services for the benefit and at the bidding of the other. (43)

The former example is particularly recalcitrant, since the fact in question concerns what *would* happen under certain circumstances, as opposed to what actually happens. Or is this just a feature of the way we describe the fact? On one view, to say that sugar is soluble in water is simply to ascribe to it a certain molecular structure; it was only ignorance of chemistry that made us put it counterfactually. In the present case, we already have another way of expressing the fact in question, viz, by saying that one of the two magnitudes is greater than the other.

This suggestion may appear facetious in view of the fact that Mill explicates the latter statement in terms of the couterfactual, rather than vice versa. But from a different point of view the order of explanation may appear to be just the opposite. Why is it possible for one magnitude to be included in the other without filling it? Because the second magnitude is greater than the first. Mill's penchant for counterfactuals is connected with his phenomenalism; recall the famous definition of physical objects as "permanent possibilities of sensation" in the *Examination of Sir William Hamilton's Philosophy*. And he clearly thinks that in the present case the counterfactual gives the correct analysis of the fact. The question is what such analysis can amount to. If facts were structures made up of objects and relations, the correct analysis would be one that revealed this structure. But this answer is not available to Mill, who takes facts as basic and generates relations—and properties, too, for that matter—out of facts and things. Strictly speaking, there are no relations on his view, only relative terms. The meaning of such a term is exhausted by its denotation, which is the thing it stands for, and its connotaion, which is a fact involving this thing. Thus there is no structure of objects and relations for the correct analysis to get right, but only things, on the one hand, and facts, on the other. All the same, it *may* make sense to say that one sentence provides a better analysis of a fact than another. In Locke's example, the sentences "*A* and *B* are related as hen and chick" and "*A* laid the egg out of which *B* was hatched" both express the same fact. But the second gives a fuller analysis of it than the first, since it mentions one more object that is involved in it, viz, the egg. Thus the latter sentence shows the fact itself to be related to an additional thing. In other cases, it may show that it is related to additional *facts*. For example, it may contain terms *connoting* these facts. This cluster of ideas will be explored in the sequel, though not precisely in the framework provided by Mill.

Peirce also identifies the foundation of a relation with a fact. He was well versed in scholastic philosophy, especially Scotus and Ockham, and it is thus possible that he formed this interpretation independently. But it seems more likely that he was led to it by Mill. For one thing, it is at best a *reconstruction* of scholastic doctrine, making it a coincidence if they came up with it separately. Moreover, Peirce was certainly aware of Mill's account, since he cites it in an article on "Relation" that he contributed to the *Century Dictionary* (1897). Finally, his treatment is identical with Mill's in all but one respect. Taking as an example a locomotive blowing off steam, he remarks that "this fact constitutes a relation between the locomotive and the steam so far as the 'blowing' is conceived to be a character of the locomotive, and another relation so far as the 'being blown' is conceived as a character of the steam." The fact itself is "the foundation of the relation." Where Peirce differs from Mill is in his view of the significance of this account. Mill thought of it as the completion of the nominalist analysis begun by his father. The essential feature of relative terms, according to the elder Mill, is that they are given in pairs. And the reason they are so given, according to the younger Mill, is "not the existence between two things of a mystical bond called a relation and supposed to have a kind of shadowy and abstract reality, but a very simple peculiarity in the concrete fact which the two names are intended to mark."[18] Peirce, on the other hand, was able to regard the very same account as the implementation of a realistic theory of relations. How is this possible? By his own admission, Peirce's brand of realism was separated from nominalism only by a hair-breadth. The nominalist's credo that abstractions are mere names would be approximately true, he said, if we struck out the "mere" (3:290). For his part, the realist has to give up the claim that they are simply real. All we are entitled to say is that they may be real and will be if they are affirmed as the final result of inquiry. This result may never be attained: it may be merely a kind of ideal limit to which theories are in the process of converging. Nevertheless, what is true here and now is defined in relation to it. This is the idealist side of Peirce. Realism ultimately reasserts itself, however, with the claim that this convergence is no accident, but is the result of laws that operate in such a way as gradually to compel assent to the ideal theory. Thus while Peirce agrees with Mill that relations are not metaphysically fundamental, he does not admit that they are therefore unreal. But to say that they are real in his sense is to say something about relational expressions, viz, that they will appear as part of the final analysis. And this, we have suggested, depends on their power to reveal interconnections among facts. "Analysis" consists not in reading off the

[18] Footnote by J. S. Mill to James Mill 1878 (7).

internal structure of a fact, but in comparing facts with each other. And the possiblility of such analysis increases as we become acquainted with more facts. This is why the reality of a given relation depends on the course of future inquiry.

Chapter 3

Bradley and the Case for Facts

The Regress Argument

Bradley's regress argument concerning relations still holds a place in the philosophical repertory in spite of critics like Broad, who judged that "charity bids us avert our gaze from the pitiable spectacle of a great philosopher using an argument that would disgrace a savage or a child." (85) Few would go so far as to maintain that the argument shows what it purports to show, yet there remains the suspicion that it reveals something other than the clay feet of its author. At the very least, it must be conceded that none of the attempts to refute it really hit the mark.

As usually stated, the argument is directed against the reality of relations. Take any relation between two terms. There will have to be further relations relating the original relation to the terms, and so on ad infinitum. Since this regress is clearly vicious, the assumption that there is such a thing as a relation between terms must be false.

There are two possible responses to this argument. One is to deny the necessity of further relations to relate the original relation to its terms. This was the solution favored by Broad, who remarked that we might as well assume the need for super glue to glue regular glue to things. The second response, which was made by McTaggart and Russell, is to deny that the regress is vicious. According to Russell (1957, 51), the relations between the original relation and its terms are implied by the proposition affirming the original relation but are not part of its *meaning*. The regress would be vicious only if they were part of the meaning of this proposition.

The distinction to which Russell appeals is too obscure to be of much help. A few pages before he introduces it, he explicitly repudiates the notion that propositions have meanings (47). *Words* have meanings, namely, the things they stand for. These, not the words, are the constituents of propositions. It seems, then, that Russell must be speaking loosely when he ascribes meaning to propositions. Instead of saying that something is or is not part of the meaning of a proposition he should have said that it is or is not a *constituent* of the proposition itself. There are then two cases. Either the proposition affirming the original relation must have as constituents the relations between this relation and its terms, and so on ad infinitum, or this is not necessary, in which case, we may suppose, the only consitituents are the original relation and its terms. Russell thought that we could rule out the first case, for reasons to be considered below. In the second case, the relation between the original relation and its terms can only be affirmed by *another* proposition, one whose constituents are those of the first proposition plus the new relation. We thus have an infinite series of propositions, each successive member of which is implied by, and is even logically equivalent to, its predecessor, but is not identical with it, since it has different constituents. If this is to be called a regress at all, it is at any rate not a vicious one, according to Russell.

There are a number of objections that could be made to this solution. For example, it is not clear that the first case can be ruled out without begging the question. Some argument is needed to show that a proposition affirming a relation does not have as constituents all of its infinite progeny. At one point, Russell argued from the premise that there is a one-to-one correspondence between the constituents of a proposition and the words in a sentence expressing it, so that a sentence expressing such a proposition would have to be infinite in length. To use his example, "*a* exceeds *b*" expresses a different proposition than "*a* is greater than *b*," since in the latter sentence "is" stands for the relation between *a* and *greater* while "than" stands for the relation between *greater* and *b* (1956, 100). Needless to say, his common sense soon reasserted itself and caused him to abandon this view. It may be thought that the first case is ruled out by the fact that *it* really does involve a vicious regress. But it has not been shown to do so. Perhaps this is supposed to be shown by the original argument, to which it is therefore conceded that if the proposition *did* have to contain all these relations its constituents would not be related at all. If so, then the second response seems to presuppose the first, since it assumes that there are propositions consisting merely of a pair of terms and a relation. If this is to be a proposition and not just a collection of elements, the relation must really relate the terms. And in order to escape the allegedly vicious first case this relating must go on without the connivance of intermediary relations.

McTaggart's version of the response (1:89) leads to much the same conclusion. Where Russell speaks of propositions, he speaks instead of facts. The difference is not merely verbal. The obvious difference between facts and Russell's propositions is that there are false propositions but no "false" facts. A more interesting and related difference is that relations *function* differently in the two cases. In a Russellian proposition the relating of the terms by the relation is what makes the proposition a unity. Since even a false proposition is a unity, a *further* explanation has to be given for the truth or falsity of the proposition. Russell, under the influence of Moore, concluded that truth and falsity are unanalyzable properties of propositions. Both he and Moore subsequently abandoned these views and with them the doctrine of propositions, substituting for it a theory of facts.[1] McTaggart's solution, then, is to posit an infinite series of facts where Russell has an infinite series of propositions. For starters, we have a fact consisting of two terms and a relation and we go on from there to ever new facts. Since the terms of a fact are related in the ordinary sense of the word by their relation, as opposed to the somewhat Pickwickian sense in which they are related in one of Russell's propositions, it is even more evident in this case that the second response presupposes the first.

Thus it all sems to boil down to whether a relation requires other relations to relate it to its terms. What are the arguments on either side? There do not really seem to be any. One strategy for "Bradley" is to get his opponent to concede—as Russell and McTaggart obligingly do—that there are relations between a relation and its terms. For having obtained this concession, he can go on to question the sense of the distinctions his opponent has to make. Is his alleged series of facts really anything but a series of increasingly full descriptions of one and the same fact? If the

---

[1] The 1906 essay "On the Nature of Truth" shows Russell still undecided whether there are propositions or only facts. The latter view is, he says, more plausible, but is faced with "formidable difficulties." Of these, the one on which he lays most stress is that one of the disjuncts of a true disjunction may be false, so that if the disjunction corresponds to a fact it would seem to be one that has a mere fiction as a part. When this essay was reprinted in the *Philosophical Essays* of 1910, the third section, in which these remarks appear, was omitted. In its place there followed a new essay in which Russell expounds his "multiple-relation theory" of belief (see Chapter 4, fn. 4). The problem about disjunction was not mentioned in the new essay, but presumably Russell would have said what he said in "The Philosophy of Logical Atomism" of 1918, viz, that there is no reason to suppose that there are disjunctive *facts* corresponding to disjunctive sentences (see the next chapter). Moore seems to have changed his mind somewhat later. In Chapter 3 of *Some Main Problems of Philosophy*, which consists of lectures given in 1910-11, he says "there certainly are in the universe such things as propositions," while in Chapter 14 he says "there simply are no such things as propositions." Moore mentions this discrepancy in the preface to the book, which was published in 1953, and offers the explanation that he may have been using the term "proposition" in different senses in the two chapters. But it seems just as likely that he changed his mind.

holding of the original relation dos not actually *consist* in the holding of a higher-order relation between it and its terms, then the connection between these relations verges on the unintelligible. But it seems that a canny opponent can simply deny the reality of such higher-order relations. By way of an argument for their necessity, it is sometimes alleged that in order for anything to count as real it must exist independently, in the manner of Aristotle's substance or the atoms of Leucippus and Democritus. To tie such self-contained entities together a relation is needed. Hence, the regress is launched as soon as relations are admitted as real. This argument is similar to one used by Bradley, but if taken out of context it is somewhat bewildering. Independence can no doubt be understood in various ways, but in general something may be said to exist independently in the intended sense if it is possible for it to exist by itself, or at any rate apart from any particular thing or set of things. This is a rather strong criterion of reality. If it were applied to Aristotle's ontology, only primary substances would be left standing. It is thus fatal to his brand of moderate realism, and indeed seems to be the main assumption behind nominalism. Certainly it was the chief bone of contention between Scotus and Ockham. As a premise in an argument against the reality of relations, it has the drawback of being harder to swallow than the conclusion. The second premise is that relations are needed to connect such independent entities. Now from the fact that two or more things exist independently it follows that each *could* exist without the others, i.e., that they are not necessarily connected. It does not follow that they are not connected as a matter of contingent fact, or that a relation is needed to effect this connection. Perhaps they hang together like the links of a chain, as Wittgenstein said (2.03). The premise becomes more plausible, however, with a somewhat more refined account of independence. For while the ability of things to *exist* each without the other may seem the ne plus ultra of independence, it is not hard to think of a case in which it would fall short of that. Suppose that Cain could exist without Abel and vice versa but that they cannot both exist without Cain's sooner or later getting around to murdering Abel. There is clearly a sense of "independence" in which Cain and Abel would not be independent. Things are independent in *this* sense only if it is possible for them to coexist without being related in any special way. This is the sense which seems to be implicit in the second premise. For if things are independent in this sense their mere existence does not suffice to account for their relatedness. Something more is required, and once this is admitted we may as well call whatever it is a "relation." Thus a case can be made for the second premise, but this premise does not by itself suffice to show the necessity of higher-order relations. The opponent need only deny the independence of relations. Indeed, Frege's doctrine of the incompleteness or "unsaturatedness" of concepts, which consists in such a denial, is sometimes presented as a solution to this problem.

Russell and McTaggart conceded that the regress would be vicious if it broke out within a single proposition or fact. They therefore denied any such possibility. When they said that there is a regress but that it is not vicious, they were talking about the infinite series of facts or propositions which they themselves posited. Since each such fact or proposition consists of various terms united by a single relation, the denial that the regress is vicious turned out to involve the denial that a higher-order relation is needed to unite a relation with its terms. But the truth of the matter is that the regress whose viciousness is disputed by McTaggart and Russell is not the regress of the original argument but rather one of their own making. The question still remains whether the original regress is vicious. If it turns out that it is not, then it will be possible to preserve the reality of relations without recourse to any dubious assumptions about how they are joined to their terms.

The alleged viciousness presumably resides in the fact that at each stage we seem to be confronted with a set of unrelated elements. The next stage always promises to relate them but ends up passing the buck. If no stage is willing to take responsibility and say "the buck stops here," then the entire collection of terms and relations remains sundered. To vary the image, if our glue lacks adhesive power there is little satisfaction in knowing that we have an unlimited supply of it.

But if we look closely we shall see that the hypothesis is not that the elements at each stage are unrelated. On the contrary, it is that at each stage the terms are related by their relation, but that this relating *consists* in the holding of a higher-order relation between the relation and its terms. The first hypothesis may be likened to the denial of composite things. Talk of such things, it is maintained, is really short for talk of their parts and the relations between them. Given this assumption, the resolution of a whole into constituents that are themselves so resoluble will give rise to a vicious regress if carried to infinity. For we never come to anything that really exists! Atomism is thus unavoidable, but only because it is built into the original assumption. To avoid it we just have to accept that the existence of a whole can consist in that of its constituents without prejudice to the reality of the whole. In exactly the same way, we can admit that terms stand in a relation without denying that their doing so consists in their having to it a higher-order relation. Once this is recognized, the regress appears to be no more vicious than that of infinite divisibility.

A few general remarks on viciousness may be welcome here. As long as the very notion of infinity was regarded as paradoxical, any regress that could not be construed as merely potential was naturally considered vicious. But as the relevant paradoxes have long since been laid to rest, there no longer seems to be any a priori reason for denying that the world contains an actual infinite.[2] If we still have occasion now and then to judge that some thesis leads to a vicious regress, this is not really a judgment about the world. Strictly speaking, the only vicious regress is a regress of explication. It occurs when the explicandum itself forms part of the explicans, and is thus hardly to be distinguished from circularity. We may profitably turn to Russell for an example:

> This form of regress commonly results from circular definitions. Such definitions may be expanded in a manner analogous to that in which continued fractions are developed from quadratic equations. But at every stage the term to be defined will reappear, and no definition will result. Take for example the following: "Two people are said to have the same idea when they have ideas which are similar; and ideas are similar when they contain an identical part." If an idea may have a part which is not an idea, such a definition is not logically objectionable; but if part of an idea is an idea, then in the second place where identity of ideas occurs, the definition must be substituted; and so on. (1956, 348)

Russell is not, of course, denying the *possibility* of two such series of ideas, a_1, a_2, ... and b_1, b_2, ..., of which each successive member is part of its predecessor. He is not even denying that in such a case a_n could be in some sense the same as b_n for all n. His point is merely that this sense has not been defined, as shown by the regress in definition.

The regress argument is usually presented in the form of an indirect proof. The infinite regress is supposed to show the absurdity of the hypothesis that relations are real. But if the view expressed in the last paragraph is correct, there can be no such proof. At most, the regress could be used to show the inadequacy of a proposed *definition* of relations, not their nonexistence. Since there is no question of *defining* relations, their reappearance at each stage is innocuous. It may be suggested that the regress *is* directed against a definition, but that what is being defined is not relation per se, or even a particular relation R, but rather what it means for an object a to have the relation R to the object b. This assumes that the assertion that terms and relation in turn stand in a higher-order relation is intended as a definition of what it is for the terms to stand in the original relation. As a definition, it is obviously inadequate, since the notion of terms standing in a relation reappears at each stage. But the failure of this definition does

[2] I have in mind such (alleged) paradoxes as that a proper part would equal the whole.

not reveal any absurdity in the notion of a relation. The argument purports to show that there are no relations, not just that they or the notion of terms standing in them are indefinable.

Split Ens

Such, at any rate, is the argument generally attributed to Bradley. On closer investigation, however, it does not seem to be the one he actually employs. The latter is directed not so much against the reality of relations, as against their ability to account for unity. This obviously calls for some explanation.

It is true that Bradley denies the reality of relations. But he does not mean by this what we meant by it in the last section, viz, that there are no relations, but only that relations, and indeed the whole scheme of relations and terms, are "appearance," as opposed to "reality," in the somewhat special sense in which he employs these terms. To call something appearance in this sense is not to deny that it exists. On the contrary, Bradley says, "What appears, for that sole reason, most indubitably *is*; and there is no possibility of conjuring its being away from it." (1899, 132) He does not just mean, as we might suppose, that it exists as an idea in someone's mind, even if nothing corresponds to it in the external world. In addition to this subjective meaning of "appearance" Bradley finds what he calls "a much wider sense," according to which "you have appearance wherever, and so far as, the content of anything falls outside of its existence, its 'what' goes beyond its 'that'." (1950a, 250) On the other hand, we have reality "so far as these two aspects are inseparable, and where one may perhaps be said to reconstitute the other."

Bradley is a little vague on the notions of content and existence, especially considering the weight they are forced to bear. The closest he ever comes to a definition is in the following passage from *The Principles of Logic*:

> For a fact to exist, we shall agree, it must be something. It is not real unless it has a character which is different or distinguishable from that of other facts. And this, which makes it what it is, we call its content. We may take as an instance any common perception. The complex of qualities and relations it contains, makes up its content, or that which it is; and, while recognizing this, we recognize also, and in addition, that it is. Every kind of fact must possess these two sides of existence and content. (1:3)

The word "fact," as used by Bradley, has various senses depending on the context. It can mean (1) any existent, as opposed to a mere content taken in abstraction, (2) a self-existent entity, i.e., a reality as opposed to an appearance, or (3) an object of immediate awareness, as opposed to a theoretical construct. In all three senses "fact" applies as much to what we should ordinarily call "things" as to facts in the usual sense. Bradley's choice of "fact" instead of "thing" as his most general term for an existent reflects his view that things are a species of fact rather than vice versa. He is critical of facts in the third sense, and this is what led Austin to say that Bradley threw cold water on facts and Wollheim to entitle two of his chapters "The Case against Facts." Here "fact" is used in the first sense, which encompasses appearances as well as realities. The *content* of a fact is a single entity consisting of a number of qualities and relations. It resembles in some respects what philosophers have called the "nature" of a thing, meaning the conjunction of all its properties regarded as a property in its own right. In much the same way, the content of a fact comprises its complete qualitative make-up. Where Bradley parts company with most philosophers, however, is in regarding the whole content as basic and the various qualities and relations as abstractions from it. Moreover, while a thing's nature consists of properties of the thing itself, the qualities and relations making up the content of a fact are not necessarily qualities that characterize the fact as a whole or relations in which it stands. Like Berkeley before him, Bradley dismissed as unintellible the notions of substance and inherence, with the result that his qualities acquire some of the characteristics of substances. For example, they are the ultimate terms of his relations. The stage is thus set for a "bundle theory" of individuals. But having disposed of substance in the second chapter of *Appearance and Reality*, Bradley goes after the bundle theory in the third. Still, he does not find equal fault with the two theories. The problem with the notions of substance and inherence is the familiar one that they depend on metaphors that can never be cashed in. An analysis in terms of them is as good as no analysis, in Bradley's opinion, and we hear no more of them once they have been weighed in the balance and found wanting. Qualities and relations are another story, since we can give *examples* of them. In spite of what he regards as their very grave shortcomings, Bradley never tires of describing them as a necessary makeshift.

Necessary, that is, if we are to have knowledge. According to Bradley, our primary experience of reality takes the form of what he calls "feeling," a state in which diversity is present but not actually distinguished. In such a state there is no such thing as truth or falsehood, and thus nothing that can properly be termed knowledge. To get that, we have to make distinctions within the whole that is presented to us. For example, we distinguish a thing's color from its shape. Part of a fact's content considered thus abstractly is what Bradley calls an "idea" or "ideal content" (1950b, 1:3) (By contrast, "content" without the "ideal" always refers to the complete nature of a fact, which suffices to distinguish it from all other facts.) Once we have an idea, we can refer it away to some fact other than that from which it was obtained. This is what is meant by "judgment," and with it comes the possibility of truth and falsehood. Bradley is here using some traditional terms with new meanings. Like Frege, he was opposed to psychologism in logic; we need only recall his famous remark that "in England at all events we have lived too long in the psychological attitude." (1:2) He fastened the blame for this attitude on the doctrine that the ideas which form the matter for judgment are "facts existing in our heads," or, as we should say, mental entities. On his view, they are not facts at all, but merely part of the content of one or more facts considered in abstraction. Talk of "abstraction" may seem to leave the door open to psychologism after all. But Bradley does not hold that ideas are *created* by abstraction, only that they are known by means of it. He was not the sort of idealist who maintains that truth is man-made; on the contrary, he repeatedly denies the coherence of any such view. (In asserting a form of distinction that is not merely intellectual but still falls short of real separability, he sides with Scotus against Ockham.)

Bradley also gives a new twist to the traditional notion of judgment. He characterizes as "superstition" the doctrine that judgment always involves a synthesis of ideas. In its most familiar form, this doctrine holds that every judgment contains two ideas, a subject and a predicate, and that the act of judging consists in combining these into a whole. (The act itself is symbolized by the copula of a sentence expressing the judgment.) Bradley views this as part and parcel of the previous error of regarding ideas as facts in the head. For only so regarded are they ours to manipulate. Against the particular form of the doctrine just mentioned he has two arguments. The first is that judgment cannot consist in the coupling of a pair of ideas, since whatever we affirm we can also doubt or deny, and it is absurd to suppose that we must first judge something to be the case before we can doubt or deny that it is so. That is, if what we deny is the very same as what we would under other circumstances affirm, and the latter can only arise from the mental coupling of a pair of ideas, which is judgment, then before we can deny something *we* must create it by joining the ideas in question, which is to say that we must first judge it to be the case. Secondly, there are judgments which it is unnatural to parse in terms of subject and predicate, for example, relational and existential judgments. Bradley concedes that every judgment can be "tortured" into subject-predicate form, but points out that in the case of "A is simultaneous with B" it is equally natural to regard either A or B as the subject "and perhaps more natural still to do neither" but rather to take the judgment as falling into two "subjects" with a relation between them. (1:22) This should serve to dispel the widespread belief that Bradley's objections to relations stem from reverence for the subject-predicate form. "It requires no great skill," he adds, "to exhibit every subject together with its attributes as the relation between independent qualities (subjects), or again even to make that relation the subject, and to predicate all the remainder as an attribute." In the latter case "exists in the case of AB" would appear as an attribute of simultaneity. Bradley speaks of greater or lesser naturalness, instead of correctness, in this connection because he does not believe that there is only one correct analysis. His point here is that the possibility of analyzing every judgment into subject and predicate does not show that every judgment is made by joining two ideas.

Bradley holds that, on the contrary, every judgment has only one idea. The fact that we can make distinctions within it does not impair its unity. Every idea, he assumes, has distinguishable aspects. Hence, if we deny the singleness of every idea that admits distinctions within itself we shall be forced to conclude that there are no ideas. The only sensible alternative as Bradley sees it, is to admit that "any content whatever which the mind takes as a whole, however large or however small, however simple or however complex, is one idea, and its manifold relations are embraced in an unity." (1:12) Of course, this argument rests on the unsupported—though by no means implausible—premise that there are no absolutely simple ideas. But Bradley also makes a more modest point. If, to use his example, we are to deny that we have a single idea of a wolf eating a lamb just because we can distinguish within it the ideas of wolf, lamb, and eating, then we should also be prepared to deny that "wolf" is a single idea, since it too admits distinctions within itself. So far there is no reason for drawing a sharp line between ideas of individuals and ideas of states of affairs.

The doctrine that judgment always involves several ideas and never just one is tied up, as we have seen, with the view that any unity to be found in it results from the act of judgment itself, which is held to consist in the relating of ideas to one another. Bradley thinks that this falsifies the role of relations in judgment:

> The relations between the ideas are themselves ideal. They are not the psychical relations of mental facts. They do not exist between the symbols, but hold in the symbolized. They are part of the meaning and not of the existence. And the whole in which they subsist is ideal, and so one idea. (1:11)

In other words, the relations are part of the subject matter about which we judge, not of the act of judging.[3] This is perhaps self-evident in the case

---

[3] For similar reasons, Bradley rejected Russell's "multiple-relation theory" of belief (see Chapter 4, fn. 4): "The view that for me, as I judge, there is no

of material relations like the eating which obtains between the wolf and the lamb. But Bradley clearly intends it to apply equally to such "formal" relations as that between wolf, lamb, and eating. His remarks here are directed primarily against ideas viewed as mental facts. But however we conceive of ideas there is a distinction to be made between (1) an idea-of-A related to an idea-of-B and (2) an idea of A-related-to-B. It is surely mere prejudice to suppose that we cannot have (2) without (1). In any case, it is (2) that is essential to judgment.

The "single idea" theory has the great advantage, in Bradley's eyes, of making good sense of judgment, a feat he considers beyond the power of those theories that make judgment a synthesis of ideas. On his view, the act of judgment consists in the attribution of an ideal content to a portion of reality. There is thus after all a sense in which every judgment has a subject and a predicate. But on the one hand, the subject is not an idea, while on the other, the predicate includes all of the content that tradition would divide between subject and predicate. Bradley takes his stand on the ground that usually at least we mean to judge about reality and not merely ideas. When we judge "this bird is yellow" we do not, he says, attribute the idea "yellow" to the idea "this bird." (1:58) Rather we attribute the whole content, which we divide into these two ideas, to a fact, in this case the bird itself. In the present example, the task of determining this fact is performed by the grammatical subject, together, of course, with the circumstances of judgment. In other cases, however, it is not possible to isolate a single part that plays this role. Bradley takes as an example the assertion "The cow which is now being milked by the milkmaid, is standing to the right of the hawthorn tree yonder." He comments:

> In this judgment we have not one thing but several, and more than one statement about their relations. But it is still a part of the presented environment which is actually the subject and the real substantive of which this whole complex is indirectly asserted.

This subject is a fact in the ordinary sense of the word. Like any other fact it has a content of its own. Our judgment is true if the ideal content which it asserts forms part of this total content. (More precisely, it has a degree of truth depending on the extent to which its ideal content approximates the total content. This is because all abstraction involves a certain amount of falsification according to Bradley. He does not argue directly for this tenet, but is content to characterize the opposite view as an unwarranted assumption. "It is a very common and most ruinous superstition," he says,

---

unity anywhere in what I take as true except the unity made by my judgment, seems indefensible." (1950a, 293).

"to suppose that analysis is no alteration, and that, whenever we distinguish, we have at once to do with divisible existence." (1:95) Referring to his own position, he observes that something "may seem ludicrous, not because it is at all absurd in itself, but because it conflicts with hardened prejudice." And it is here that we must leave the matter.)

Granted that the true subject of our judgment is a portion of reality and no mere idea, how is this reference to reality secured? Not by ideas alone, insists Bradley:

> When we say "It rained last Tuesday," we mean *this* last Tuesday, and not any other; but, if we keep to ideas, we do not utter our meaning. Nothing in the world that you can do to ideas, no possible torture will get out of them an assertion that it is not universal. (1:63)

It may be objected that, on the contrary, all we need is an idea that applies to just one thing. For then we can form a judgment about this thing by means of a definite description. Bradley considers a specific form of this objection in which relations in time and space are trusted to yield such an idea. For example, last Tuesday may be the day on which some unique event occurred. As Bradley is quick to point out, this presupposes that such events can be found, which they could not if, say, the doctrine of eternal recurrence were true. We may not take this possibility very seriously, but it does show that any ability we may have to refer by means of ideas alone is purely fortuitous. In any case, a thing does not stand in the same spatio-temporal relations in every possible world. And from this Bradley concludes that our idea does not determine its object absolutely but only relative to the way the world is. In order to determine it absolutely it would have to distinguish it not only from all other actual objects but from all other possible ones as well. If we rely on the world to supply a unique reference, then we have only traded our original problem for that of distinguishing the actual world from all other possible worlds on the basis of mere ideas. This is impossible in principle if any of these worlds should happen to be qualitatively indiscernible from the actual world. In any case, it is impossible in practice for finite intellects such as ours.

According to Bradley, it is only our immediate contact with reality that permits us to refer to it. In regard to series of events in time and space he writes:

> It is not by its quality as a temporal event or phenomenon of space, that the given is unique. It is unique, not because it has a certain character, but because it *is given*. It is by the reference of our series to the real, as it appears directly within this point of contact, or indirectly in the element continuous with this point, that these

> series become exclusive. We perhaps may be allowed to express this otherwise by saying, it is only the "this" which is real, and ideas will suffice so far as "thisness," but can never give "this." (1:64)

Bradley goes on to explain that it thisness falls within the *content*, as opposed to the existence, of a fact, whereas the *this* always goes beyond it. He admits, and even insists, that the *idea* "this" is, like all ideas, universal. The same goes for "here," "now," and "mine." Readers of the *Phenomenology* will recall that Hegel made a similar point about demonstratives (60). No matter how hard we try, he said, we can never make them refer to unique individuals. For example, this evening we write "Now it is night." If "now" really referred to this evening, then our statement would remain true when we read it tomorrow at noon. But to Hegel it is obvious that it would not. A contemporary philosopher might deny that tonight's truth and tomorrow's falsehood are the same statement, in spite of the fact that a single sentence suffices for both. Hegel was hampered in this regard by the assumption that a term has the same reference in every context. If this reference is not a particular, then, he reasoned, it can only be a universal. If Bradley learned this doctrine from Hegel, he did not draw the same lesson from it. Hegel wanted to show that we can only judge of universals, however much our facility with concepts like "this," "here," and "now" may give us the illusion of judging directly of fact. Bradley, on the contrary, was fully persuaded of our ability to judge of fact, but set his face against any attempt to account for this ability in terms of ideas alone. In this respect, he maintained, demonstratives are like other ideas, as much as they may differ from them in other ways.

Bradley's remarks on demonstratives are mostly confined to "this," but he gives to understand that they also apply mutatis mutandis to the rest. Considered as a universal, *this* is the property of being sensibly present to me or, alternatively, of being the focus of my attention. (1:69) Bradley seems to favor the former alternative but thinks it does not matter much which we adopt. In either case, *this* is not a quality of the object but rather a relation of the object to the judging subject. Its claim to universality resides in the fact that it remains the same amid a change of the object perceived or attended to. But if *this* is like other ideas in being universal, it nevertheless differs with respect to the role it plays in judgment. Unlike most ideas, says Bradley, it does not function as a "symbol." By this he means that it does not form part of that ideal content which, in judging, we attribute to a portion of reality. Thus when we judge of a certain animal "This is a wolf," we only characterize it as lupine and not also as sensibly present or as occupying our attention. In such a judgment we *use* our relation to the object to secure uniqueness of reference, but it forms no part of the subject matter about which we judge. "This," according to Bradley, merely deputizes for the object itself:

> In every judgment, where we analyze the given, and where as the subject we place the term "this," it is not an idea which is really the subject. In using "this" we do *use* an idea, and that idea is and must be universal; but what we *mean*, and fail to express, is our reference to the object which is given as unique. (1:66)

When Bradley says that we fail to "express" our reference, he means only that we do not succeed in putting it in general terms, not that it remains in any way indeterminate. It is determined by the fact that we stand in a certain unique relation to the object. Bradley's point is simply that we must guard against leaving this fact out of the equation and supposing that the abstract relation alone suffices for reference.

In spite of his emphasis on our immediate contact with the real Bradley is not of course suggesting that we can only judge of the here and now. Judgments that are so restricted are styled "analytic" in his admittedly heterodox nomenclature, on the ground that they only analyze the given. By contrast, "synthetic" judgments are any that transcend the here and now. They too inherit their reference to reality from our contact with it, though in their case it is secured indirectly, the fact of which we judge being specified in terms of its relations to the fact with which we are in contact. For example, when we judge that it rained last Tuesday we mean the last Tuesday up to *now*.

Nor does every judgment, according to Bradley, fit the simple pattern we have been discussing, in which a specific ideal content is ascribed to a limited portion of reality. Strictly speaking, this pattern applies only to judgments which assert a property of an individual or a relation between two or more individuals, and perhaps to conjunctions of such judgments. Of those judgments that do not fit the pattern the most important in Bradley's estimation are the hypotheticals. In a hypothetical judgment the ideal content is divided between antecedent and consequent, neither of which is actually asserted. What is asserted, we suppose, is rather a relation between them. But how are we to conceive of the terms of this relation? Not as facts, clearly, since the relation may hold even if antecedent and consequent are both false and thus do not represent facts. Nor, in general, can these terms be taken as ideal contents, since both antecedent and consequent may contain demonstratives and thus fail to be purely qualitative. Bradley admits that a judgment like "if he had murdered he would have been hanged" may assert only "the general connection of hanging with murder," in which case "the 'he' is irrelevant." (1:89) On the other hand, the judgment "If this man has taken that dose, he will be dead in twenty minutes" leaves it open whether "the dose would poison anyone, or would only poison such a man as he is, or would not even poison such a kind of man, unless under present special conditions." It does not assert a relation between ideal contents but between states of affairs involving this man and that dose. But Bradley does not let it rest there. Our aim, he insists, is to characterize reality, not some merely possible states of affairs which have no part in it. So he comes back again to the idea that in judging we ascribe a quality to the real. In a hypothetical judgment, however, the quality does not explicitly appear. Bradley compares such a judgment to an imaginary experiment of which the antecedent gives the conditions and the consequent the result. What is affirmed is neither the conditions nor the result nor the connection between them, but, as he puts it, "the mere ground of the connection; not the actual existing behavior of the real, but a latent quality of its disposition, a quality which has appeared in the experiment, but the existence of which does not depend on that experiment." (1:87) This quality remains to a certain extent occult, so that it may not be possible to determine without further investigation whether another judgment asserts the same quality or a different one. The real subject to which it is attributed is correspondingly indeterminate and often, it seems, not to be distinguished from reality as a whole. But Bradley does not maintain, as is sometimes alleged, that the latter is the invariable subject of judgment. It is true that he relegates anything short of the whole to the sphere of appearance. But he never denies that we can judge regarding appearances.

This brings us back around to the original pretext for this digression. The given is never self-contained, according to Bradley. On closer examination it will always be found to be what it is only in relation to other facts that are not given. (This appears to be an empirical generalization.) These relations are part of its content. We are able to judge of the given without taking them into consideration only because we do not rely upon content alone to single out our object. But our ability to discriminate an object from the general background is no guarantee that it is really separable. Bradley takes this dependence upon a greater whole as the defining characteristic of appearance. It is this he has in mind when he says that something is an appearance if its content falls outside its existence. It has nothing to do with appearing *to* anyone, aside from the fact that, according to Bradley, that which appears always does in fact display such dependence. (For independent reasons, he holds that *everything* is experience. This is no less true of reality than it is of appearance, however, and thus could not be used to define the latter.) Thus the fact of a wolf's eating is appearance, whether anyone perceives it or not, since it is impossible to eat without eating *something*. Because he holds that everything is internally related to everything else, Bradley concludes that anything short of reality as a whole is appearance. But it is not contained in the definition of appearance that this is the case.

E Pluribus Unum?

"This is the doctrine for which I have now for so many years contended." So writes Bradley (1:112, fn. 50) in the second edition of *The Principles of Logic*, published two years before his death. He is referring to the conclusion of the regress argument as it appeared in the first edition of that work, the first of several occurrences in his writings. Specifically, the conclusion is that "relations exist in and through a whole which can not in the end be resolved into relations and terms." We find it stated more fully in the last piece of philosophy Bradley wrote, an unfinished article on relations which was published posthumously in the *Collected Essays*:

> From terms taken as in themselves unrelated, and from a relation not taken as itself their relation, there is no logical way to the union present in, and required for, the relational fact. What has to be accounted for has hence so far been simply ignored. And while we keep to our terms and relation as external, no introduction of a third factor could help us to anything better than an endless renewal of our failure. (2:643)

These statements show that the argument to which Bradley attached such great importance is not the reductio ad absurdum of relations canvassed in the first part of this chapter. That argument was seen to be invalid because it treated an infinite regress as tantamount to a logical contradiction, when in fact no regress is vicious except in the context of an attempted explanation. A vicious regress occurs when the thing to be explained keeps cropping up in the process of explaining it. It is not a question of truth—every statement in the series may in fact be true—but of explanatory adequacy. This is clearly the way Bradley views the matter when he describes the regress as an endless renewal of *our* failure to *account* for the unity of the relational fact.

What is really at stake here is the ontological status of facts. Are they analyzable without residue into their constituents, or must they be acknowledged as irreducible entities in their own right? What distinguishes a fact from a mere assortment of separate items is the connection existing among its constituents. Indeed, nothing seems to stand in the way of our identifying the fact itself with this connection. But we must not think of the latter as an abstract relation like the eating that unites not only this wolf and that lamb but any pair consisting of eater and eaten. The word "relation" is ambiguous as between this and the more concrete sense of a being related. It is in the latter sense that the judgment "the wolf is eating the lamb" may be said to affirm a relation between the wolf and the lamb; it does not affirm the abstract relation of eating, whatever that might entail. In contrast, "connection" can only mean a being connected. There is not the same temptation to think of it as an additional *thing* that does the connecting. The connection is not a constituent of the fact; it is the fact itself.

Bradley's point is simply that any attempt to reduce a fact to terms and relations will either leave their connection out of the picture entirely, thereby missing what is most essential, or will wind up reintroducing it at a higher level. In the latter case we have only exchanged one fact for another; we have made no progress towards the reduction of facts to more basic entities. Thus, given the wolf, the lamb, and the relation of eating, we do not yet have a fact. In the first place, the three things may be totally unconnected. And in the second place, even if we assume that they are connected, the way in which they are connected remains indeterminate: perhaps the lamb is eating the wolf. At this point we may have recourse to a higher-order relation. But if we mean by this a *concrete* relation like that affirmed by the judgment "the wolf has the relation of eating to the lamb," then we are appealing, not to a mere relation, but to a fact, and we are no better off than when we started. If, on the other hand, we mean the *abstract* relation of having that also figures in other facts besides this one, then all we have done is add one more item to our original set of things to be connected. We are thus embarked on a regress.

The objections to the previous argument do not apply to this one. On the one hand, the regress is clearly vicious, since our whole object is to give an analysis of facts. On the other hand, we cannot avoid it simply by saying that it is the nature of relations to relate things, just as the nature of glue is to stick them together. This objection had some force against the previous argument, which turned on the alleged necessity of a higher-order relation to relate a relation to its terms. It was hard to see what could decide this issue one way or the other. But it is curiously irrelevant to the argument presently under consideration. For granted that it is the nature of a relation to relate, the question is how to account for its relating these particular things in this specific way. Similarly, glue sticks things together without the aid of super glue, but not unless a dab is actually present between the relevant surfaces. Frege's doctrine of properties and relations as incomplete or "unsaturated" entities is sometimes presented as a solution to Bradley's problem. It does provide an answer of sorts to the question how a relation is able to connect its terms without the aid of a higher-order relation. The answer is that the relation is just what is left over after a pair of objects is figuratively removed from a larger whole, so that a pair of objects is all that is required to make it complete again. But this doctrine offers no solution to the problem of accounting for facts in terms of their constituents, since the order of explanation is here just the opposite: from wholes to the relations that appear in them, instead of vice versa.[4] For the same reason, the problem is not solved by saying that a fact is a function of its constituents. For all this means is that there is a function that has a fact as its value whenever that fact's constituents are taken as arguments. And this presupposes that there are such things as facts to make up the range of this function.

In the last chapter we saw Ockham using an argument similar to Bradley's. His object was to show that the connection existing between things is nothing over and above the things themselves. As he saw it, the question is where to draw the line. If we can stop the regress at the second step by simply denying the need for anything to connect a relation to its terms, then we ought to be able to stop it already at the first step by denying the necessity of the relation itself. And plurality is not to be posited beyond necessity. Bradley also considers it unnecessary to go past the first step, but his starting point is different from Ockham's. Since what has to be accounted for is the union of things into wholes, he starts out with a whole and asks whether it can be reduced to its constituents. When he finds that it cannot, he concludes that we are stuck with it. Ockham, on the other hand, starts out with an assortment of objects and argues that the addition of further objects such as relations does not help to account for their connection. Where he goes wrong is in concluding that therefore the original objects must already suffice to account for it by themselves.

According to Bradley, this could only be the case if the objects in question were taken as internally related. By this he means treating one object as including in itself a relation to another. But to treat it in this way is already to regard it as a fact, since all we mean by a fact is a connection between things. In the same way, as we have already seen, if we take the relation as a concrete relation involving its terms, we are taking *it* as a fact. Bradley's doctrine of internal relations is one of the most misunderstood aspects of his philosophy. He does not maintain that all relations are internal, and even describes as "ludicrous" the ascription of

---

[4] Frege, of course, was fully aware of this. The doctrine of unsaturatedness was for him merely a consequence of the doctrine that states of affairs or propositions are more fundamental than their constituents. Subsequent philosophers who have taken the former doctrine out of context, whether for praise or blame, have misunderstood it. See Chapter 4 below.

any such view to himself. (2:642) What he does maintain is that relations, as well as the terms they relate are only an abstraction from the relational fact as a whole. We have a certain amount of freedom in choosing how much of the fact gets apportioned to a given term. As Bradley puts it:

> The question in every case is as to how far your selection has been carried. How much of the fact, that is, has it abstracted and fixed within an individual term, and secured so that you can take it as your term's essence? Any relation involved in that result will be intrinsic. And, on the other hand, where any relation goes beyond that special limit, it will belong to the term only so far as that is taken as in one with the whole relational fact, and will so far be external. (2:646)

Thus we can make a relation internal or external more or less as we please. Bradley himself suggests that it was his polemic against merely external relations that led to his being branded a proponent of internal ones. But that polemic was really directed not so much against external relations per se as against the attempt to reduce facts to such relations and their terms. By contrast, internal relations were so obviously parasitic upon facts that a "reduction" to them held little attraction.

Some of the misconceptions about Bradley's views are due to Russell. Despite a series of exchanges remarkably free of polemics, neither man really succeeded in grasping the other's position. But Russell's misunderstanding of Bradley has been far more influential than the latter's misunderstanding of him. On the issue with which we are concerned, however, we find them in agreement. In 1904, in a review of Meinong, Russell writes:

> The unity of a complex raises a logical problem, of which Meinong seems to be not fully aware. What is added, we are told, is the relation, rightly related; but when we consider the relation as well as the terms, we do not obtain the complex. And if we add the relations of the relation to the terms, and all the relations generated in the resulting endless process, we still do not obtain again our original unity, but only an aggregate. Thus what distinguishes our complex is not any constituent at all, but simply and solely the fact of relatedness in a certain way. (1973, 28)

This is essentially Bradley's regress argument. Though Russell had tried to refute the argument, construed as an argument against relations, the year before, the real point must have registered subliminally. Under the circumstances, it is scarcely surprising that Bradley was somewhat perplexed. The terms "internal" and "external" also proved a stumbling block. By and large, Bradley used the latter term for what I have been calling an abstract relation, as opposed to a concrete connection between things. His point was that we cannot account for unity purely in terms of such relations and their terms, which is just Russell's point above. He did not deny that it is sometimes useful to speak in terms of such relations. Nor did he describe his view as a theory of internal relations. Russell did that. And by internal relations Russell meant ones that are essential to the things standing in them. He took Bradley to be maintaining that all relations are internal in this sense. Bradley, on the other hand, thought that Russell was saying that all relations are external in *his* sense:

> Mr. Russell's main position has remained to myself incomprehensible. On the one side I am led to think that he defends a strict pluralism, for which nothing is admissable beyond simple terms and external relations. On the other side Mr. Russell seems to assert emphatically, and to use throughout, ideas which such a pluralism surely must repudiate. He throughout stands upon unities which are complex and which cannot be analysed into terms and relations. These two positions to my mind are irreconcilable, since the second, as I understand it, contradicts the first flatly. (1950a, 281)

If there is a real disagreement between Bradley and Russell, it is on the issue of holism. Russell, while acknowledging the irreducibility of facts, nevertheless thought of them as taking a back seat to the individuals and relations making them up. For Bradley, on the other hand, individuals and relations were abstractions from concrete facts. This theme of atomism and holism will be further developed in the next chapter.

Chapter 4

The Two and the Many

> Every apparently separate piece of reality has, as it were, hooks which grapple it to the next piece; the next piece, in turn, has fresh hooks, and so on, until the whole universe is reconstructed.
>
> (Russell, describing Hegel's doctrine of internal relations)

> Frege actually drew this conclusion; and he meant it in an almost metaphysical sense, reminding one somewhat of the Eleatic doctrine of the "One." "The True"—according to Frege's view—is analyzed by us in different ways in different propositions; "the True" being the name he uses for the common signification of all true propositions.
>
> (Gödel, on the "Slingshot")

The Time Bomb

One of the underlying principles of Frege's theory of sense and reference is that the reference of a complex expression depends only on the objects referred to by its parts and not on the way in which these objects are referred to. This principle can be seen as underlying the doctrine of indirect reference, for example, since it entails that where the reference of a sentence depends on the ordinary sense of a part, this sense must be the reference of that part in that context. According to Frege, it also underlies the doctrine that sentences refer to truth values. For it guarantees that the reference of a sentence will remain unchanged when a constituent expression is replaced by another expression having the same reference. And what besides the truth value, asks Frege, "belongs quite generally to every sentence if the reference of its components is relevant and remains unchanged by substitions of the kind in question?" (1977, 64) The obvious implication is that the truth value is the only thing that remains constant amid all such substitions. It remained for Church (1956, 24) to turn this into an explicit argument. Consider the following sentences:

(1) Sir Walter Scott is the author of *Waverley.*

(2) Sir Walter Scott is the man who wrote twenty-nine Waverley Novels altogether.

(3) The number such that Sir Walter Scott is the man who wrote that many Waverley Novels altogether is twenty-nine.

(4) The number of counties in Utah is twenty-nine.

Since (2) is obtained from (1) by replacing "the author of *Waverley*" by another expression referring to the same thing, (1) and (2) refer to the same thing on Frege's principle. (Note that the fact that "Waverley" occurs in both expressions is merely a coincidence from a logical point of view. We could just as well have written "author of *Ivanhoe*" in place of "author of *Waverley*" in (1). The point is simply that both expressions refer to Scott.) The same principle applies to (3) and (4), where "the number of counties in Utah" is substituted for an expression referring to the same number. With regard to (2) and (3), Church says that these are either synonymous, i.e., that they have the same sense, in which case they have a fortiori the same reference, or at any rate that the difference in sense is too slight to affect the reference. Thus, by the transitivity of identity, (1) and (4) have the same reference, even though the only relevant thing they seem to have in common is that they are both true. Of course it does not follow from this one example that any two true sentences must have the same reference. Nor does Church provide any general recipe for constructing a similar argument given an arbitrary pair of true sentences. He claims only that enough similar examples could be given to make Frege's conclusion at least plausible. And indeed, if we go along with the rest of the argument, it is rather hard to get off at this point. For the discovery of further examples requires only ingenuity and an almanac. And it would be idle to insist upon sorting true sentences into many equivalence classes instead of just one, when the principle of classification is so mysterious as to class together sentences like (1) and (4).

If this argument is sound, then Russell was wrong when he said that facts are "the sort of things that you express by a sentence." He meant that true sentences correspond to facts, not that they name or refer to them. But it makes no difference what we call the relation in question, so long as it depends only on what the parts of a sentence refer to and not on the way in which they refer. The same argument would also rule out Russell's earlier theory, according to which sentences have such a relation to what, following Moore, he called "propositions." These propositions resemble the facts of his later theory, inasmuch as, e.g., the proposition that the earth revolves around the sun is, like the homonymous fact, a complex object consisting of the earth, the sun, and the relation of revolving around, and not, as with Frege's "thoughts," of senses or other intensional entities referring to these things. The chief, or sole, difference between facts and Russellian propositions is that there is also, e.g., a proposition, but no fact, that the sun revolves around the earth. Some such notion appears to have been in the air at the turn of the century, since it is also what Meinong meant by an "objective."

Indeed Frege himself originally held a similar theory, until considerations like the above caused him to have second thoughts. In *Begriffsschrift* and *The Foundations of Arithmetic*, which were written before he made the distinction between sense and reference, sentences correspond to what he called "judgable contents" (*beurtheilbare Inhalte*), because they are the objects of the act of judgment. The exact nature of the correspondence is complicated slightly by the fact that, as Frege sees it, sentences of ordinary language already contain an element of assertion, and thus express the act of judging itself along with the content judged, so that if we simply want to refer to the latter we should use phrases like "the circumstance that" or "the proposition that" followed by the sentence, or else a noun phrase like "the violent death of Archimedes at the capture of Syracuse," instead of the actual sentence "Archimedes perished at the capture of Syracuse." (1977, 3) In Frege's symbolic language, assertion is indicated by putting a vertical line in front of an expression for a judgable content. He suggests that the same division of labor could be achieved in ordinary language by writing, e.g., "the violent death of Archimedes at the capture of Syracuse is a fact." And in general Frege prefers to paraphrase expressions like "$\vdash A$" and "$\nvdash A$" as "A is a fact" and "A is not a fact," respectively, rather than as "A is true" and "A is false," which already suggests that he thinks of judgable contents as states of affairs, as opposed to something like the thoughts of his later theory. This is borne out by the fact that the "unjudgable contents" which form the constituents of judgable contents include such things as the earth and the sun, and not just senses referring to such things. Moreover, the relation between an expression and its content would appear to coincide with the later relation of reference in the case of singular terms, since it simply associates the expression with an object. And just as in the later theory two different expressions can have the same reference but express different senses, so in the earlier theory they can have the same content but determine it in different ways. The notion of a way of determining an object is the doctrine of sense in embryo.

Perhaps it would be closer to the truth to say that the relation between an expression and its content just *is* the relation of reference, but that between the earlier theory and the later Frege was forced to revise downwards his estimate of the number of objects available to serve as contents (references) of sentences. From this point of view the later theory merely adds a superstructure of senses and reduces the number of judgable contents to two. This was apparently Russell's view of the matter, since he says in an appendix to the second edition of *Principia Mathematica* that according to Frege there were only two propositions, one true and one false. (1:659) Frege himself described the truth value of a sentence as "the circumstance that it is true or false," thereby appropriating to truth values the standard way of designating judgable contents. (1977, 63) It is significant in this connection that he spoke of the parts of a sentence as referring to parts of its truth value, just as he had previously spoken of unjudgable contents as parts of judgable ones. To be sure, he adds that such a way of speaking can be attacked. (65) But he does not repudiate it, and the main objection he raises against it, viz, that the whole and one part do not suffice to determine the remainder, applies to judgable contents as well as to truth values. Both cases involve that sense of "part and whole" in which, according to Frege, a function and its argument are parts of the value of the function for that argument.

Here the function is what Frege called a "concept" (*Begriff*), which is the content of a predicate in the earlier theory and its reference in the later one. In the earlier theory concepts are functions from objects to judgable contents. (Higher-order concepts, such as the quantifiers, are functions from concepts to judgable contents.) If we view the later theory as simply shrinking the category of judgable contents to the two truth values, these become functions from objects to truth values, which is what concepts are in the later theory. There is nothing that would lead one to suppose that concepts in the earlier theory are functions in intension, whereas those in the later theory are functions in extension. While it is only in *The Basic Laws of Arithmetic* that Frege explicitly states that concepts having the same extension are the same, an extensional view of functions in general is implicit in his earlier writings. For the only relevant facts about a function are what values it assumes when "completed" with what arguments. He would undoubtedly have scorned the suggestion that the way in which the value is computed has anything to do with functional identity. (It is true that in *Begriffsschrift* functions are to all appearances purely linguistic, but they are also defined in such a way that it is impossible for two distinct functions to have the same value for the same argument.) If the predicates "is human" and "is a featherless biped" correspond to the same concept according to the later theory, but to different ones according to the earlier, this is due, not to differing criteria of functional identity, but to the fact that these functions always take the same value for the same argument on the later theory, while on the earlier theory they always take different ones. Thus both functions take Socrates into the True according to the later theory, but into the circumstance that Socrates is human and the presumably different circumstance that he is a featherless biped according to the earlier. In effect, the later theory identifies the contents of sentences having the same truth value, and in the process identifies all functions that differ only with respect to those contents.

From the standpoint of the later theory, Frege came to view his earlier notion of content as a kind of unstable compound of sense and reference, and spoke of separating these elements. (1964, 38) But when speaking in this way he had in mind *judgable* content, which in retrospect seemed to conflate thought and truth value. It is only after sense and reference are distinguished on the sentential level that parts of sentences appear to require sense as well as reference. And then the reason is that the thought expressed by a sentence naturally depends on the parts of which the sentence is composed, and cannot depend only on the *reference* of these parts, since it may change if one of them is replaced by another expression having the same reference. Frege could not very well claim to have discovered that his former notion of *un*judgable content also conflated sense and reference, since content and reference are identical in the case of singular terms, while in the case of predicates the difference between them is to be attributed to the different ranges of the functions, and not to any element of intension allegedly present in the content and needing to be purged therefrom to yield the reference.

Originally, then, Frege held what would now be termed a theory of direct reference for all types of expressions, though he used the word "content" instead of "reference." I think that he switched to the later theory of sense and reference because of his seeming discovery that sentences with the same truth value cannot differ in reference. For obviously truth values are not individuated finely enough to serve as objects of judgment or account for our differing cognitive relations to sentences in the way that the old judgable contents could. As Frege said, "we can never be concerned only with the reference of a sentence," given that sentences refer to truth values. (1977, 65) His solution was to shift the burden of individuation from reference—where it had been placed by the earlier theory—to the way in which the reference is determined, a strategy that might be styled "intensional ascent." The notion of a way of determining an object had been around since *Begriffsschrift*, where it was invoked to render more palatable the thesis that identity is a relation between names. But not until the later theory are these ways of determining objects recognized as objects in their own right under the name of "senses."

What I wish to suggest is that this recognition is a result of the identification of sentence reference with truth value, and not vice versa as is generally supposed. As I see it, the need to posit sense arises first at the level of the sentence as a whole, whence it is communicated to the parts.

This is contrary to the prevailing view according to which the distinction between sense and reference was introduced in order to solve a puzzle about identity and applies in the first instance to singular terms. That view receives its imprimatur from the fact that Frege himself presented the distinction in this way in his well-known essay on the subject. But as Descartes pointed out, the order of discovery is not necessarily the most suitable order of presentation. The conclusion that sentences can only refer to truth values is, to say the least, rather a surprising one, and Frege may well have felt that the reader would be more willing to follow him out onto that particular limb once the safety net of sense was already in place. In any case, I do not believe that the puzzle in question is what prompted the distinction. Frege already had what he considered a satisfactory solution to the former that did not depend upon the latter.

The puzzle and its solution are among the most familiar facets of Frege's philosophy, thanks to their prominent placement in "On Sense and Reference." Frege begins that essay by inquiring whether identity is a relation and, if so, whether it is a relation between objects or between names of objects. Curiously, the former question, once raised, is never really considered; it is simply taken for granted that identity is a relation of some sort. (This already suggests that the whole topic of identity functions as little more than a kind of rhetorical hook.) In *Begriffsschrift* Frege had assumed that it is a relation between names, and he rehearses here his reasons for that assumption. On the one hand, the sentences "$a = a$" and "$a = b$" are said to differ in "cognitive value," since the former is a priori, whereas the latter may be used to report an empirical discovery, e.g., that the morning star is the same as the evening star. On the other hand, "if we were to regard equality as a relation between that which the names 'a' and 'b' designate, it would seem that $a = b$ could not differ from $a = a$ (i.e., provided $a = b$ is true)." (1977, 56) The meaning of this second statement becomes clearer once we realize that in *Begriffsschrift* a difference in cognitive value must reflect a difference of judgable contents. These are the objects of judgment and thus of cognition. But, on the assumption in question, "$a = b$" has the same judgable content as "$a = a$," vi, the circumstance that a is self-identical. If the difference of names is to be relevant to what is judged, then the names themselves, and not just the objects named, must be part of the content of judgment. Thus Frege concluded that, when connected by the identity sign, names stand not for their contents but for themselves. (This would not be the last time he employed the device of systematic ambiguity.) This meant, of course, that the identity sign itself had to be taken as signifying sameness of content rather than actual identity, since we do not mean to assert that "a" is the same as "b."

It was at this point in *Begriffsschrift* that Frege introduced the notion of a way of determining an object. He was concerned lest this treatment of identity make it appear "as though it were here a matter of something pertaining only to expression, not to thought; as though we had no need of two symbols for the same content, and therefore no need of a symbol for equality of content either." (1977, 11) This is exactly what Wittgenstein later concluded. But according to Frege it overlooks the fact that different names may correspond to different ways of determining the same object, so that a judgment of identity, though concerned with names, is not concerned only with names. He has in mind the kind of situation in which one and the same geometrical point may be characterized as the point of intersection of lines a and b as well as that of lines b and c. (Actually, this example is taken from "On Sense and Reference" (57), where Frege uses it to illustrate the notion of a "mode of presentation." In *Begriffsschrift* (11) he gives a more elaborate example, also geometrical, in which a line rotates around a point on the circumference of a circle until it is tangent to the circle, at which time its point of intersection with the circle is the same as the point around which it is rotating. So here too it is a matter of two different ways of characterizing one and the same point. The similarity of the two examples leaves no room for doubt that the later notion of a mode of presentation, and thus of a sense, grows out of the earlier one of a way of determining an object.) It is the way in which a name determines its content and not the name per se that really matters to judgment. At one point Frege goes so far as to say that the content of a judgment of identity is "*that*, in a particular case, *the same* content actually is given by *two ways of determining* it," i.e., as opposed to the two different names. But he immediately adds that before we can make this judgment "we must supply, corresponding to the two ways of determination, two different names for the thing thus determined." (11) Why should he have deemed this a necessity? If the different ways of determination are what really count, why can we not judge directly of them and eliminate the middle man? Once they are admitted as senses, we can. But at this stage Frege seems to have been unwilling or unable to contemplate them as entities in their own right, sans linguistic clothing. Was it mere ontological puritanism that made him turn his back on *Sinn* at this time?

Frege's examples suggest that by the way in which a name determines its content he means the way in which it presents it as the value of a function for one or more arguments.[1] If we write "$f(x, y)$" for "the point

[1] Baker and Hacker argue that this is also what he means by sense (301ff.) But they admit that it does not account for everything he says about the later notion, e.g., that even simple names have senses. For this reason, it seems to

of intersection of lines x and y," then "$f(a, b)$" and "$f(b, c)$" have the same content, viz, a certain geometrical point, but determine it in different ways, i.e., as the value of the function f for different pairs of arguments. According to Frege, the division into function and argument "has nothing to do with conceptual content; it concerns only our way of looking at it." (14) There is thus no way back from content to way of determination.

We might hope to get the way of determination into the content of judgment by judging about the functions and arguments themselves instead of about either their values or the names of those values. This would eliminate the linguistic middle man. But it is easier said than done. Suppose we try to interpret the statement "$f(a, b) = f(b, c)$" as stating that the result of completing the function $f(x, y)$ with a and b is the same as the result of completing it with b and c. This would amount to a new analysis of the content of this statement, according to which it would be of the form $P(f(x, y), a, b, c)$, where P is the appropriate higher-order concept.

The problem is not with the analysis as such. On Frege's principles, the content of any statement can be analyzed in an indefinite number of ways. What is present only as a function on one analysis may figure as an argument on another, as in the present case. (In particular, this is true when the function in question is a concept. The content of the statement "Socrates is mortal" may be analyzed into Socrates and the property of being mortal, or into the latter property and the higher-order property of being a property of Socrates, or into this higher-order property and the still-higher-order property of being a property of mortality; there is no end to this kind of leapfrogging. While this is a rather trivial-looking way of generating alternative analyses of a judgable content out of a given analysis, it is essential to the treatment of generalization in *Begriffsschrift*. In *The Foundations of Arithmetic*, Frege considers much more radical examples, such as the claim that "line a is parallel to line b" has the same judgable content as "the direction of line a equals the direction of line b." (76))

The problem is precisely that this *is* just one analysis among many. It involves taking the expressions "the result of completing $f(x, y)$ with a and b" and "the result of completing $f(x, y)$ with b and c" as incomplete symbols having no content by themselves. But it is also possible to break the sentence up in such a way that these become names of the values in question. And when this is done, the sentence appears to state that these values are one and the same. In other words, we are back where we

---

me better to say that, while it is undoubtedly the germ of the notion of sense, it does not represent its full fruition. Once senses are posited as entities in their own right, what might formerly have counted as a definition becomes a partial elucidation.

started, asserting that a certain point is self-identical. We cannot judge directly about the way of determination of an object without at the same time judging about the object, because the way of determination is in a sense transparent. In order to judge about it we must do so indirectly, by judging about a sign that corresponds to it. Signs have the requisite opaqueness.

I think that this was Frege's main reason for supposing that names are necessary for judgments of identity. It is one that would apply up until the introduction of senses. But in *Begriffschrift* he may have had another reason as well. For the account of functions in that work involves an apparent confusion of use and mention:

> Suppose that a simple or complex symbol occurs in one or more places in an expression (whose content need not be a possible content of judgment). If we imagine this symbol as replaceable by another (the same one each time) at one or more of its occurrences, then the part of the expression that shows itself invariant under such replacement is called the function; and the replaceable part, the argument of the function. (1977, 13)

Strictly speaking, this is a definition, not of functions, but of expressions thereof. In "Function and Concept," Frege remarks that this is a mistake to which mathematicians are peculiarly prone, not mentioning that he had previously been guilty of it himself (22). And a number of commentators have sought to exculpate him or at least to mitigate the charge. But one would search *Begriffsschrift* in vain for evidence that by "function" he means anything but a kind of expression. To the uncaptive eye his theory at this early stage was that, while both the whole and the replaceable part he calls the argument are expressions with contents of their own, the part he calls the function is a kind of syncategorematic expression having no independent content. Thus a way of determination cannot exist apart from a name, and this is another reason why names are necessary for judgments of identity. The functional void is at least partially filled in *The Foundations of Arithmetic.* Although functions in general are not discussed in this work, concepts, which are functions from objects to judgable contents, are. And here we are told, for example, that a relational concept is what remains of a *judgable content* when we subtract from it a pair of *objects* (82). So by this time, if not before, we find Frege holding the now familiar doctrine that the division of an expression into what he would later call saturated and unsaturated parts corresponds to a similar division *in re.* Yet this apparently does not lead him to repudiate the account of identity given in *Begriffsschrift*, so that of the two explanations just given for the necessity of names in identity judgments the first would seem to be the more important.

Why *did* Frege repudiate his early account of identity? The standard view is that he did so for reasons given in the following passage:

> What is intended to be said by $a = b$ seems to be that the signs or names "a" and "b" designate the same thing, so that those signs themselves would be under discussion; a relation between them would be asserted. But this relation would hold between the names or signs only in so far as they named or designated something. It would be mediated by the connection of each of the two signs with the same designated thing. But this is arbitrary. Nobody can be forbidden to use any arbitrarily producible event or object as a sign for something. In that case the sentence $a = b$ would no longer refer to the subject matter, but only to its mode of designation; we would express no proper knowledge by its means. But in many cases this is just what we want to do. If the sign "a" is distinguished from the sign "b" only as object (here, by means of its shape), not as sign (i.e., not by the manner in which it designates something), the cognitive value of $a = a$ becomes essentially equal to that of $a = b$, provided $a = b$ is true. A difference can arise only if the difference between the signs corresponds to a difference in the mode of presentation of that which is designated. (1977, 57)

In order to read this as an argument against the account of identity statements given in *Begriffsschrift*, we should have to suppose that by the time he wrote this Frege had forgotten what he said in that work about ways of determination. For the whole point of that discussion was to deny that on his view identity is a relation between signs considered purely as shapes.

Needless to say, he did *not* forget all this, and this is not an argument against his earlier account. What we have here is rather a *restatement* of that account. As in *Begriffsschrift*, Frege is concerned to avert the criticism that he is making identity a purely linguistic matter. There it took the form of a contention that if his view were correct the identity sign would be redundant, since having two signs for the same content is a luxury we can always do without. Here he approaches the subject from a different angle. If the sentence "$a = b$" simply stated that the shape "a" is used as a sign for the same thing as the shape "b," then, he says, "we would express no proper [i.e., non-linguistic] knowledge by its means." Suppose we find someone who has never encountered the names "Hesperus" and "Phosphorus" (and is ignorant of Greek) and inform him that they refer to the same thing. Frege's point is that if this is all we tell him, we could just as well say that "Hesperus" refers to the same thing as "Hesperus," for all the good it does him. They are just sounds as far as he is concerned, and the connection of sounds with things is purely arbitrary. The picture changes if he is able to associate the sounds with different ways of getting at the object by way of its relations to other things. Then the sounds become different *signs.* Frege is here making the same point as he made in *Begriffsschrift.* There the different ways of getting at the object were called "ways of determination," whereas here they are called "modes of presentation." So far from repudiating his former account of identity statements, he is using it as a pedagogical bridge to the general notion of sense. If by the end of the essay the emphasis on names has more or less evaporated, it is because ways of determination have now been promoted to the status of full-fledged entities, under the name of senses, whereas before they were mere aspects of expressions. It was always the way of determination, and not the expression, that mattered to judgment, but up to now we couldn't have the one without the other. The reason for this promotion is not, however, dissatisfaction with the former account of identity statements, for no such dissatisfaction has emerged. Frege had no difficulty accepting that such statements, though apparently concerned with objects, are really about names. He could not with the same equanimity accept *sentences* as the objects of judgment. But when it transpired that sentences refer to their truth values, it was either this or emancipate the mode of presentation of the truth value from the sentence expressing it. And once this was effected, the general emancipation of modes of presentation was assured.

This account also provides an answer to another question. Senses and ordinary things (using the term loosely to include truth values and functions) are like oil and water. Their modes of interaction are severely limited. Are there functions taking ordinary objects into thoughts, for example? Frege does not say. Given his picture of function and argument as parts of the function's value for the argument, an affirmative answer would seem to imply that an object like Mount Etna can be part of a thought, which he denies (1980, 79). Perhaps this is to stress unduly a metaphor about whose tensile strength Frege himself had his doubts. Be that as it may, senses form a layer over and above ordinary objects and concepts, and their nature is left somewhat mysterious. It would obviously be better if they could be identified with more familiar kinds of entities. And at first it looks as if this can be done. Within the framework of *Begriffsschrift* there are entities that appear ideally suited for the task, viz, concepts. Of course, since the most important characteristic of senses is that they *determine* their references, not just any concepts will do, but only those that are satisfied uniquely. Thus the sense of "Aristotle" would have to be some concept applying exclusively to him, such as *taught Alexander.* The question is why Frege did not avail himself of this opportunity. And the answer provided by the above account is this. He could avail himself of it only on the assumption that concepts are functions from objects to judgable contents, as in *Begriffsschrift.* For on that assumption *taught Alexander* and *invented formal logic* are different concepts, since they take the same object into different judgable contents, and thus we can have different senses referring to the same object, as required. But if the above account is correct, that train had already left the station by the time Frege got around to introducing sense. Judgable contents had already become truth values, and concepts had changed accordingly. They were now functions from objects to truth values. A concept applying uniquely to Aristotle was a function assigning the True to Aristotle and the False to everything else. There could not be more than one such function.

Frege himself ascribed this leveling effect to the principle of substitutivity. To what extent did he have Church's argument, or something like it, in mind? There can be little doubt that he would have accepted this argument if it had been presented to him. For besides the principle of substitutivity all it asks us to assume is that sentence (3) refers to the same thing as sentence (2). Frege could hardly have denied this. As we have seen, he was ready to attribute sameness of content to sentences that apparently differ much more radically from one another than these do, e.g., "line *a* is parallel to line *b*" and "the direction of line *a* is the same as that of line *b*." He held that two sentences have the same content if they always yield the same consequences when taken together with the same additional premises (1977, 2). Furthermore, the chief difference between (2) and (3) is that "twenty-nine," which is used attributively in the former, is the subject of the latter. Frege explicitly licenses such transformations in *The Foundations of Arithmetic*, attributing the same content to the sentences "Jupiter has four moons" and "the number of Jupiter's moons is four." (69)

Thus even if he was not aware of the argument himself, it was like a time bomb ticking away in the foundations of his early theory. When it went off, it would level the entire structure of judgable contents, leaving only two props standing. Senses would then be required to provide a new roof. (On the larger philosophical stage, this is exactly what did happen. Unmindful of the explosion over at the Frege place, philosophers continued to erect structures out of the same materials, i.e., facts or Russellian propositions, until Church ignited the gunpowder Carnap had inadvertently stored in the basement of his *Introduction to Semantics.* When Carnap turned to the task of rebuilding, he employed intensions resembling Fregean senses.) There are, however, a number of ways of getting from the principle of substitutivity to the conclusion that sentences refer to truth values. We shall consider some of these in the next section. Any of them would suffice to vindicate Frege's claim, though his own argument is too enthymematic to enable us to say with much confidence which he intended. Perhaps he simply came to realize that by gorging on definite descriptions a sentence can burst any prima facie constraints upon its content. After all, a given thing can be described uniquely in indefinitely many ways, and to each description there corresponds a sentence with a content of its own, which seems to form part of the content of any sentence in which the description occurs. It is hard to deny, for example, that part of the content of (2) is that someone wrote twenty-nine Waverley Novels altogether. And if, as in this case, the sentence was obtained from another by substituting the description for a coreferential singular term, the principle of substitutivity will step in to assure us that the new content was already present in the original sentence. If we imagine the process of substitution as continuing indefinitely, it is easy to believe that all true sentences will converge on the same total content, what we might call the True. This becomes all the more plausible when we realize that any true sentence can be embedded in a definite description without affecting the reference of the latter.

We introduced judgable contents by comparing them to Russellian propositions. The point of comparison was that like the latter they have ordinary things as constituents, instead of senses. But there is an even more striking point of *contrast*, and it is this that accounts for the instability of the Fregean notion. Russell's account of propositions was atomistic, in the sense that he thought of them as being built up out of elements, i.e., things, properties, and relations. They are thus structured entities, which are identical only if they consist of the same elements combined in the same way. Frege, on the other hand, started with judgable contents and arrived at their parts by analysis. Since there may be more than one way of splitting a given whole up into parts, we cannot automatically assume that a difference of parts signifies a difference of wholes. This holism of Frege's is in symbiosis with his view of concepts as functions.[2] For the representation of something as the value of a function for a given argument or arguments makes no pretense of being unique. The number 12 can be represented as $7 + 5$, or as 3×4, or in an indefinite number of other ways, e.g., as the number of the Apostles. Similarly, if the relation of concept to judgable content is simply that of a function to its value, there is no reason to expect a unique representation of the latter in terms of the former. Indeed, if *every* such function is to count as a concept, there will always be infinitely many representations of any given judgable content: we need only consider the constant function with the given content as value for every argument.

---

[2] Both themes figure prominently in the recent books by Sluga and Baker and Hacker. The former regards Frege's holism as a legacy of German idealism and his view of concepts as its formal implementation. According to the latter, Frege's leading idea was the application of function theory to logic, and the holism falls out as a consequence.

Perhaps Frege would not have counted this function as a concept.[3] But in any case his treatment of generalization required a modicum of flexibility in the analysis of judgable contents, to account for the fact that we can infer both "someone killed someone" and "someone killed himself" from "Brutus killed Brutus." And, as we have seen, the mixing of concepts and ordinary functions throws the doors wide open. For in Church's example we have a function that takes us from Scott to the content of (1) and another function that takes us from the number twenty-nine to Scott. Hence the composite of the two functions takes us from twenty-nine to the content of (1).

But surely the instability of judgable contents cannot be blamed entirely on their representation in terms of functions and arguments? After all, this is how we represent numbers, and there is no temptation to collapse all of *them* into, say, zero and one. The comparison with numbers is instructive. One main difference is that in their case we have a privileged form of representation in terms of the successor function. Questions about the identity of numbers can be settled by reducing both sides of an equation to this canonical form. Without it, we should be free to entertain all manner of hypotheses, e.g., that different expressions always refer to different numbers, or that all refer to the same one. Additional information might enable us to rule out some of these hypotheses. For example, we might know that every number is either odd or even, but not both, and that certain expressions refer to odd, and certain others to even, numbers. That would rule out the hypothesis that all expressions refer to the same number, but leave open the possibility that they all refer to one of two, which we might call the Odd and the Even. Frege had little more to go on in the case of sentences, but, miraculously, this little was enough to rule out every hypothesis but one. How was this possible?

Where there is a privileged representation of objects in terms of functions and arguments, this representation enables us to say what the object

---

[3] I argued above that concepts are functions in extension. This has to do with their identity conditions. We now see that there is an equally important question about their *existence* conditions. If the former question has to do with whether the correspondence between concepts and functions is one-to-one, the present one has to do with whether it is onto. In the case of the "propositional functions" of *Principia Mathematica*, the answer to both questions is "no." That is, they are not only functions in intension, but also not every function from objects to propositions counts as a propositional function. In the case of Ramsey's "propositional functions in extension," which he introduces in "The Foundations of Mathematics" (52), the answer to both questions is "yes." He points out that for such a function ϕ, "ϕ(Socrates) may be Queen Anne is dead," while "ϕ(Plato) may be Einstein is a great man." I do not know how Frege would answer the second question.

consists of. In this sense, the number two consists of the number one and the successor function. If we substitute "seven minus six" for "one" in the expression "the successor of one," the resulting expression still stands for two by the principle of substitutivity. But this does not mean that six and seven are "constituents" of two in the sense that one is. The canonical representation allows us to recognize them for what they are, namely, auxiliary objects introduced in order to *specify* one of the constituents. Frege denied that there is always a single correct analysis of a judgable content into constituents. This is what I called his holism. It implies that there is also no privileged representation. But it does not imply that all representations are on a par. Frege's tendency to view functions and arguments as parts of their values may have misled him in this regard. To pursue the metaphor of carving up a physical thing, there are an indefinite number of ways of slicing an apple, but none of them yields orange slices. Similarly, there may be things that are definitely *not* constituents of a given state of affairs. A representation that relies on these things will be a more or less external representation as opposed to one in which only constituents are involved. It thus ought to be an open question whether twenty-nine is a constituent of the content of (2) or only an auxiliary object, and thus whether or not (2) has as part of its content th circumstance that someone wrote twenty-nine Waverley Novels altogether. But Frege does not treat it as such. Instead, he takes the absence of a privileged representation as implying that every object or concept invoked by a sentence is a full-fledged constituent of its content. And this is almost unavoidable if we insist that a unique content be recoverable from every sentence. For if we have only (2) to go on, what reason can we give for excluding twenty-nine from its content? If (2) says only that Scott is the author of *Waverley*, or indeed that Scott is Scott, what do we do if we want to say that he is the man who wrote twenty-nine Waverley Novels altogether?

The alternative seems to be to admit that sentences like (2) are ambiguous, perhaps multiply so, depending on whether objects like twenty-nine are treated as constituents or merely as what I have called auxiliary objects. We shall consider this solution in the next section. Frege could perhaps have accepted it as applied to ordinary language, which was admittedly full of ambiguities. But his symbolic language was intended to be unambiguous. It would thus have been necessary to indicate, perhaps by parentheses, as in arithmetic, that, e.g., "the man who wrote twenty-nine Waverley Novels altogether" must be evaluated before the rest of (2), if (2) is obtained from (1) by substitution. Then, when "the number of counties in Utah" is substituted for "twenty-nine," it will appear inside these parentheses, where it can do no harm. But it would be idle to speculate on Frege's possible reaction to this suggestion.

To the extent that Frege's holism rests upon the fact that representations in terms of functions and arguments are not unique, it is obviously built on sand. For unless we are able to swallow the metaphor of functions and arguments as parts of their values, we shall still find it necessary to make invidious distinctions between different representations of the same content. Frege himself understood the limitations of this metaphor, but was probably unwilling to jettison it outright because his account of the difference between functions and objects depended on the notion of unsaturatedness. But his holism is plausible quite apart from all this. There is a *very* often quoted remark of Kreisel's to the effect that what matters is not so much whether there are mathematical objects as whether mathematical statements are objective. Frege thought that we have a better purchase on whether our statements are objective than on what they are about. And he was surely right about this. We are much more certain of the truth of the statement that England went to war with Argentina than we are of its proper analysis. And while this does not prove that it has no single correct analysis, it makes the possibility worth entertaining. Russell tended to think in terms of relations instead of functions.[4] Whereas Frege regarded relations as a species of functions, Russell regarded functions as a species of relations, viz, as ones that relate every first term to a unique second term. This explains many of the differences between their ontologies. For example, a relation either relates a pair of terms or it does not. This made it rather hard for Russell to account for the unity of a false proposition,

---

[4] In *Principia Mathematica*, to be sure, relations are contextually defined in terms of propositional functions. But it is not always noticed to what an extent the philosophical arm of that work takes back what the mathematical one has given. The relations that are defined in terms of propositional functions are relations in *extension*, i.e., entities standing to polyadic predicates as classes stand to monadic ones. (They are not reduced to classes, however, as in set theory, but are on a par with them.) The elimination of classes and relations in favor of propositional functions is the so-called "no-class theory." But what are propositional functions? Although Russell has a tendency to confuse them with *expressions*, as Frege (1980, 83) was one of the first to point out, they are best regarded as functions to propositions. But—hold on to your seat—there are no such things as propositions! There are only *facts*, which in *Principia* are called "complexes." And these are made up of objects, properties, and relations. Propositions are eliminated from any context in which they might appear by the "multiple-relation theory" of belief, according to which, e.g., Othello's belief that Desdemona loves Cassio is a relation, not between Othello and the proposition that Desdemona loves Cassio, but between Othello, loving, Desdemona, and Cassio. This assumes that the only contexts in which propositions need appear are belief contexts.

since it could not consist in the fact that the relation which is asserted to hold actually holds. And this put pressure on him to deny propositions in favor of facts. On the other hand, since Frege's relations are functions, each of them must assign a value to every pair of arguments of the appropriate type. For example, the greater-than relation must be defined for 1 and 0 as well as for 0 and 1. So there will automatically be objective falsehoods, and, in the later theory, even the False itself. And just as functions encouraged Frege's holism, so relations naturally favored Russell's atomism. For unlike functions, relations do not pass away without a trace, leaving only their "value" behind. We always have a structure consisting of the relation and its terms. And if we want to identify two such structures with the same fact, we must do so explicitly.

I am not alone in maintaining that the distinction between sense and reference results from Frege's introduction of truth values as the references of sentences. A similar view is also put forward by Baker and Hacker in their book *Frege: Logical Excavations.* Some of their arguments seem to reinforce mine. First, they point to the fact that concepts are already identified with functions to *truth values* in "Function and Concept." Since this essay preceded "On Sense and Reference," they consider it reasonable to assume that the innovations that appear in it are "prior, both temporally and logically, to the elaboration of the sense/reference distinction." Unfortunately, this argument is undermined to some extent by the fact that Frege alludes to the distinction in "Function and Concept" and even refers in this connection to "On Sense and Reference," which is described as forthcoming in the journal in which it eventually appeared. (1977, 44) Baker and Hacker are aware of the first point at least. They rightly point out that the distinction plays "only the most minimal role" in the former essay. Nevertheless, it is there. Secondly, they cite Frege's statement in *The Basic Laws of Arithmetic* that "concept and relation are the foundation stones" on which he builds, seeing in it "a strong *prima facie* case that he saw the sense/reference distinction as an adjunct of his redefinition of concepts and relations in the *Basic Laws*, not as the ultimate philosophical foundation of his logical system." (237) They are undoubtedly right about the negative point. The foundation of that system, as they have argued persuasively, is the doctrine of concepts as functions in *Begriffsschrift.* The distinction between sense and reference is little more than an embellishment.[5]

But the question is what led to this embellishment. I have essentially argued from the principle of sufficient reason. The introduction of truth values as the references of sentences would provide a sufficient reason for making the distinction. The puzzle about identity would not, for the

---

[5] A fact previously remarked upon by Anscombe and Geach (162).

reasons given above. (Baker and Hacker assume that Frege *is* arguing against his earlier account of identity statements at the beginning of "On Sense and Reference," though they find his argument "opaque" (285).) But the chief difference between my account and theirs concerns the reason for introducing truth values in the first place. According to Baker and Hacker, it is in order to forge a purely *logical* connection between concepts and their extensions (272). This was allegedly necessary in order to reduce arithmetic to logic along the lines indicated in *The Foundations of Arithmetic*, where numbers are identified with the extensions of certain concepts. If a concept is a function from objects to truth values, then its extension is essentially the class of objects to which it assigns the True.[6] On the earlier theory there was no such logical route from the concept to its extension, since the value of a concept was a judgable content. The range of the concept of being mortal includes both the circumstance that Socrates is mortal and the circumstance that the number two is mortal. To determine the extension of this concept, we should have to know which circumstances are factual, and this, it is claimed, is no longer a matter of pure logic.

This explanation is highly attractive. But it is not the reason Frege himself gives for introducing truth values. *He* says that we are forced to introduce them by the principle of substitutivity, and I have taken him at his word. This account, moreover, is not without attractions of its own. On Baker and Hacker's view, truth values have to be *postulated* as the references of sentences in order to make a go of logicism. They view all of Frege's *arguments* for this conclusion as inconsequential. But good arguments, by his lights, are to be found where he says they are. Furthermore, Frege originally thought that the notion of the extension of a concept was eliminable from the definition of number in favor of the concept itself (1950, 80 fn.). And while he appears to have ultimately reconciled himself to the necessity of extensions, he does not appear to have done so until after the introduction of truth values.[7] This makes it unlikely that considerations having to do specifically with extensions were responsible for such a fundamental shift. Finally, the benefits obtained by replacing judgable contents with truth values could be obtained equally well by the less radical expedient of dividing them into facts and fictions.

---

[6] I am ignoring the complication that extensions are courses of values instead of classes.

[7] Burge, who discusses this question at length, concludes that between 1891 and 1892, "Frege was still working out the implications" of substituting concepts themselves for their extensions in the definition of number (28).

The Slingshot

Recently, facts have been making a comeback on the philosophical stage, under the direction of Barwise and Perry. According to them, the world is the totality of "situations," which consist of individuals having various properties and standing in various relations. Both holistic and atomistic conceptions find a place in their theory. On the one hand, situations themselves are regarded as ontically and epistemically prior to individuals, properties, and relations, which are said to arise as "uniformities across situations" (1983, 50). On the other hand, situations are *modelled* in the theory by structures composed of such elements, much as numbers are modelled by sets, without actually being sets. Such a structure may model a situation completely, only partially, or not at all. If it gets anything at all about the situation wrong, then it does not model it at all, just as an otherwise perfect model of the natural numbers would be disqualified if it had two zeros. A partial model of a situation gets everything right as far as it goes, but it does not necessarily go all the way. In this sense, a model of the natural numbers might be a partial model of the real numbers. A partial model is said to "classify" a situation, whereas a complete one is said to "correspond" to it (61). Utterances are interpreted in terms of these models, and their truth or falsity is explained in terms of whether or not the models in question classify situations. Not surprisingly, then, Barwise and Perry are concerned to refute Church's argument, which they refer to as the "slingshot," presumably because of its snappiness.

Logical Equivalence. Frege did not provide a criterion of identity for judgable contents, and probably thought that no such criterion was possible. To be sure, he said that two judgments have the same content if they always have the same consequences when combined with the same other judgments as additional premises. But he did not think that we could know the consequences of a judgment without first knowing its content. He did not, after all, have a model-theoretic conception of logical consequence. Thus in the last section we had to compare sentences (2) and (3) with paradigms in Frege's writings to show that he would probably have accepted Church's claim that they refer to the same thing. Frege aside, that claim can be seen as the weak link in the argument, resting as it does on the alleged sameness or near-sameness of meaning of the sentences in question. But perhaps by combining Frege's idea that logically equivalent sentences have the same content with the modern understanding of logical equivalence we can strengthen it.[8]

[8] Barwise and Perry (1981, 396) seem to think that this is what Church had in the back of his mind, but was prevented from saying by the fact that he

This is the approach taken by Davidson, who employs the argument for various ends in various places. The version employed in "True to the Facts" (752–3) is interesting because it is couched in terms of correspondence instead of reference, showing that the problem is not just with the assumption that sentences refer. It is also appropriately "Eleatic" in its conclusion, viz, that all true sentences correspond to the same fact, which Davidson calls "The Great Fact." In addition to the principle of substitutivity, he takes as a premise that "the fact that P" refers to the same fact as "the fact that Q" if P and Q are logically equivalent. Then, where S and T are any true sentences, he offers the following derivation:

(1) "S" corresponds to the fact that S.

(2) "S" corresponds to the fact that $\iota x(x = \text{Diogenes} \,\&\, S) = \iota x(x = \text{Diogenes})$.

(3) "S" corresponds to the fact that $\iota x(x = \text{Diogenes} \,\&\, T) = \iota x(x = \text{Diogenes})$.

(4) "S" corresponds to the fact that T.

Here (1) rests on the assumption that true sentences correspond to facts. Since "S" is logically equivalent to "$\iota x(x = \text{Diogenes} \,\&\, S) = \iota x(x = \text{Diogenes})$," (2) follows from (1) by the principle about logical equivalence.[9] (3) follows from (2) by substitutivity, since "$\iota x(x = \text{Diogenes} \,\&\, S)$" and "$\iota x(x = \text{Diogenes} \,\&\, T)$" both refer to Diogenes. And (4) follows from (3) by the principle about logical equivalence again.

Davidson's argument is more general than Church's, since, if sound, it shows that an *arbitrary* pair of true sentences correspond to the same fact.[10] But it stands or falls with the assumption that logically equivalent sentences correspond to the same fact, if any. And according to Barwise and

---

was writing an introduction and had not yet introduced the notion of logical equivalence.

[9] To see why "S" is equivalent to the identity statement in (2), assume a "Fregean" theory of descriptions, according to which a description refers to the unique object described, if there is one, and otherwise to some object outside the universe. (We shall see that adopting Russell's theory of descriptions is a way of avoiding the slingshot.) Then if "S" is true, both definite descriptions refer to Diogenes, and so the identity statement is true as well. But if "S" is false, then the first description refers to an object outside the universe and the second refers to Diogenes, so that the identity statement is false too.

[10] Church, however, had given an equally general argument in his review of Carnap's *Introduction to Semantics*.

Perry this assumption would be unacceptable in the first place to anyone at all sympathetic to the idea that sentences correspond to facts (1983, 25). For they see the modern notion of logical equivalence as depending, historically at least, upon Frege's identification of a sentence's reference with its truth value. Sentences are defined as logically equivalent if they have the same truth value under all assignments to their non-logical constants. This means that "John is sleeping" is logically equivalent to "John is sleeping and Mary is either weeping or not weeping." But according to them, no one would suppose that these sentences represent the same fact, since they differ in subject matter, the second, unlike the first, being about Mary.

I think that Barwise and Perry overstate their case. We do not have to go out of our way to find a philosopher who would have viewed both these sentences as representing the same fact. As is well known, Wittgenstein held that tautologies like "Mary is either weeping or not weeping" do not picture facts at all. Where does this leave sentences like "John is sleeping and Mary is either weeping or not weeping," which have tautologies as parts? According to Wittgenstein, "the logical product of a tautology and a proposition says the same thing as the proposition," and "therefore, is identical with the proposition." (4.465) This sentence thus expresses the same proposition as "John is sleeping," and would picture the very same fact, if it pictured a fact at all. (The qualification is needed because only atomic propositions picture facts, and "John is sleeping" would not be an atomic proposition for Wittgenstein. But the conjunction of a tautology and an *atomic* proposition pictures the same fact as the atomic proposition.) It only appears to be about Mary. Why would anyone hold such a view? Ramsey, who shared it, appealed to the conviction that the conclusion of a logical inference must "be in some sense contained in the premises and not something new," and recorded his inability to believe "that from one fact, e.g., that a thing is red, it should be possible to infer an infinite number of different facts." (146)

Both Ramsey and Wittgenstein were concerned to deny that logical constants like "not" and "and" refer to constituents of facts.[11] Wittgenstein even described this denial as his "fundamental idea" in the *Tractatus*.

---

[11] Ramsey's remarks were explicitly directed against Chadwick's "Logical Constants." Chadwick's theory might be viewed as a generalization of Russell's "multiple-relation theory" of belief to other propositional operators. On his analysis, the sentence "B is red and D is square" corresponds to a "conjunctive fact" consisting of a *tetradic* relation of conjunction and the four terms B, redness, D, and squareness. Similarly, the fact that B is not larger than D "is to be analyzed into B, larger than, D, and a triadic relation of negation which holds between B and larger than and D." Ontologically, this theory is not without its attractions. Like Russell's theory of belief, it eliminates reference

(4.0312) He observed that if "not" stood for such a constituent, the double negation of a sentence would represent a different fact from the sentence itself, since it would have different constituents (5.44). Ramsey explained why this would be bad. If p, not-not-p, not-not-not-not-p, etc. all stood for distinct facts, then their equivalence would have to be explained by postulating a relation among these facts, which would be no explanation at all. Wittgenstein also argued along similar lines from the interdefinability of the logical constants. But what clinched the matter was the apparent redundancy of any facts other than atomic ones. For the totality of atomic facts settles the truth value of every atomic proposition and thus of every molecular one. An atomic proposition is false if it does not picture any of the atomic facts.[12]

In a manner of speaking, Barwise and Perry admit conjunctive and negative facts, though they do not treat "and" and "not" as referring expressions. What they call a model of a situation is a set of sequences of the form $(r, x_1, \ldots, x_n, i)$, where r is an n-ary relation, $x_1, \ldots, x_n$ are objects,

---

to objective falsehoods or merely possible states of affairs in favor of properties, relations, and individuals. Every fact, moreover, is of the same basic form, consisting of an n-ary relation and n terms. (Quantifiers are treated as higher-order properties.) But, as Ramsey points out, it makes the application of logic something of a mystery.

12 Russell held that this form of explanation covertly employed negative and general facts. For that the atomic facts in question are all there are is a general fact, and that a given proposition does not picture a given atomic fact is a negative one (1971, 236, 213). Wittgenstein himself says that "the world is determined by the facts, and by their being *all* the facts." (1.11) But he does not consider this last to be itself a fact. On the contrary, he regards statements about all facts as nonsense, on the grounds that *fact* is a pseudo-concept (4.1272). Nor is it a fact, according to him, that a given proposition does or does not picture a given fact. This is something that is *shown* by the proposition in question, but if it were a fact it could be said, and thus *could* not be shown (4.1212). This doctrine is hard to swallow. As Russell observes in his introduction to the *Tractatus*, Wittgenstein "manages to say a great deal about what cannot be said, thus suggesting to the sceptical reader that possibly there may be some loophole through a hierarchy of languages, or by some other exit." (xxi) Russell himself argues from the existence of true negative and general statements to corresponding facts. But in any case not every true statement can correspond to a fact. Consider, for example, the statement "This sentence does not correspond to a fact." The assumption that it corresponds to a fact leads to a contradiction. It follows that it does not correspond to a fact, so that what it says is true. Again, having created atomic facts, must God create *another* fact in order to make them be *all* the atomic facts? Or is it sufficient for him to abstain from further creation?

and i is 0 or 1.[13] If $i = 1$, then $x_1, \ldots, x_n$ stand in the relation r in the model, while if $i = 0$, they do not. Thus the sequences may be regarded as atomic facts and negations thereof, and the model itself as a conjunction of one or more such facts.

Negative facts have been a subject of controversy at least since 1914, when by his own account Russell almost caused a riot at Harvard by teaching them (1971, 211). Demos, who was in the audience at the time, later put forward a rival theory according to which not-p asserts the existence of a positive fact incompatible with p. I have nothing to add to the long, inconclusive debate that has gone on since. As regards Barwise and Perry, however, it seems to me that their theory could accommodate a more or less "Demotic" treatment of negation, should that prove desirable. In their book they develop a theory of "constraints," which are themselves facts about the relations of implication or incompatibility between types of situations. Thus not-p could be taken as asserting the existence of a situation and a constraint that together preclude p. An alternative would be to deny that a sequence of the form $(r, x_1, \ldots, x_n, 0)$ is necessarily isomorphic to any part of a real situation. It might only serve to classify such situations as incompatible with the holding of r among $x_1, \ldots, x_n$. In that case, to be sure, any model *corresponding*—in Barwise and Perry's sense—to such a situation would have to contain, say, a sequence $(s, x_1, \ldots, x_m, i)$ that was incompatible with $(r, x_1, \ldots, x_n, 1)$, or two or more sequences that together were incompatible with it, etc.

As regards conjunctive facts, various reasons might be given for admitting them, apart from the bad one that they are needed to give conjunctions something to refer to. According to Barwise and Perry, we *perceive* that some situations are parts of others. For example, everything going on at a given spatio-temporal location is a situation, and is part of everything going on at a larger spatio-temporal location. It still might be maintained that all we are perceiving are the atomic situations, and that these alone are real, were it not for one thing. We have no experience of such atomic situations, and for all we know there aren't any. If every situation is divisible into further situations, we seem to have no choice but to admit the reality of wholes as well as parts.[14]

"But his abstaining would *make* it a fact!" It would make it true, I admit. But if not every truth corresponds to a fact, the air of platitude is sucked out of this objection.

13 I am leaving out certain complications that are not relevant to my purposes.

14 Wittgenstein also thought that we are unacquainted with atomic facts, and relied on a form of transcendental argument to prove their existence. Like other examples of the genre, however, this argument seems to me to be unsound.

By exploiting the above features of situations, Barwise and Perry are able to assign different interpretations to sentences like "John is sleeping" and "John is sleeping and Mary is either weeping or not weeping." The former will be true in any model containing the sequence (sleeping, John, 1), whereas the latter will only be true in those containing both this sequence and either (weeping, Mary, 1) or (weeping, Mary, 0). Since many models will contain the same sequence or sequences, the relation between sentences and models will not be the one-to-one relation of correspondence assumed by the slingshot. But this is an unrealistic assumption to start with, and to the extent that the slingshot incorporates it, it is being used for pot shots at a strawman (the same one that Strawson took on in his debate with Austin.) For while arguments can be given for admitting *con*junctive facts, disjunctive ones are another story. The disjuncts cannot be parts in the way conjuncts can, since, as Russell pointed out, one of the disjuncts may not exist at all. Since a disjunction is less determinate than its disjuncts, *it* is more like a part of each of them. But this really won't work either, since it would mean that the fact that John is sleeping or Mary is weeping would be part of the fact that John is sleeping, and thus every fact would involve everything in the world, something we would like to get away from if at all possible.

A more realistic assumption is that facts are what make sentences true when they are true, and this relation between sentences and facts is many-to-many. This calls for a rewording of the assumptions of the slingshot. Sentences differing in the prescribed ways must be assumed to be *made true* by the same fact*s*, if any, instead of corresponding to the same fact. It is not clear that the assumptions come through the operation with their plausibility intact. The principle of substitutivity in particular derived its plausibility from the idea that the names occuring in a sentence refer to constituents of the corresponding fact, while the sentence itself shows how these constituents are put together. Replacing one name by another was supposed to make no difference, so long as the thing named remained the same, since we should simply be replacing a constituent with itself. It now appears that sentences are more like general terms that *characterize* facts than singular terms that refer to them.[15] But presumably so long as they characterize

---

[15] There may, to be sure, be other ways of referring to facts. Clark and Fine put great store in the possibility of doing so by means of expressions in nominal position, e.g., by means of phrases like "the fact that S" or by means of variables. But if what we have said is true, there is a question how to interpret the former. "The fact that S" can hardly refer to the unique fact that makes S true, since there will generally be many facts that do so. What is intended seems to be the *least* such fact under the partial ordering of the part-whole relation. But in some cases, there will be no least fact. The fact that P or

them by specifying some of their constituents and some of the relations between them, the above rationale will still hold good. At least I shall assume that this is the case when I return to the principle of substitutivity below.

One casualty of the proposed rewording, however, is the "Eleatic" corollary to the effect that there is only the one Great Fact. For all we are now entitled to conclude is that all true sentences are made true by the same fact*s*. But while it is interesting to note that the corollary depends in this way upon the assumption that sentences have a one-to-one relation to facts, this can provide but little comfort to the proponent of facts. For even if there should be many facts instead of just one, the argument seems to show that they are indiscernible by sentences of our language. In that case, it would be idle to insist that they are distinct.

Barwise and Perry's point seems even more reasonable when viewed as a point about what makes sentences true, as opposed to one about their interpretations. For the sentence "John is sleeping and Mary is either weeping or not weeping" could hardly be true if there were *no* facts about Mary. How could Wittgenstein have thought that it says the same as "John is sleeping," when the latter sentence, unlike the former, could be true if Mary didn't even exist? Given his assumptions, Wittgenstein had a good answer to this. For he thought that the objects out of which facts are composed exist eternally and necessarily (2.024-2.0271). This means that if Mary were an object in his sense, it would be impossible for her not to exist, and so to say that she is either weeping or not weeping would do nothing to narrow down the possibilities. And this, in Wittgenstein's eyes, would be tantamount to saying nothing at all. Now Mary would almost certainly not count as an object in this sense.[16] But in that case, "Mary" is a covert description, and when fully analyzed, "Mary is weeping" and

---

Q will be the same as the fact that P, if P is true and Q is false. But what if both P and Q are true? There is no reason to prefer the fact that P over the fact that Q, and it would be arbitrary to take the fact that P *and* Q, which is larger than either. The problem is not limited to overt disjunctions. Putnam says somewhere that "jade" is used to refer to two entirely different chemical substances. Thus the fact that a is jade will be either the fact that a is F or the fact that a is G. This is in itself no problem, since presumably nothing can be both F and G. But there may well be predicates F—among the many whose analysis is unknown—such that being F is being G or H or both. This means that expressions like "the fact that S" will frequently fail to refer.

16 Wittgenstein argued that there *must* be such objects in order for propositions to have a determinate sense (2.021-2.0211). He apparently felt that this absolved him of the onus of saying what they are like, as indeed it would if his proof were sound.

"Mary is not weeping" will be mutually contradictory sentences in which only such objects are mentioned. Hence there will *necessarily* be facts making one or the other of these sentences true. Their disjunction will thus be necessary in this rather strong sense. But this result comes with a big metaphysical price tag, since it presupposes that facts about contingent existents are reducible to facts about necessary ones; in other words, that there are no contingent objects, only contingent facts.

On the other hand, if we regard Mary as an irreducibly contingent *object*, then "Mary is either weeping or not weeping" is not necessary in the strong sense of there necessarily being facts making it true. How can this be, when it is *logically* true? The answer has more to do with semantics than metaphysics. The standard semantics for extensional logics presupposes that all proper names refer, so that every model of a language must assign an object to each of them. Thus "Mary is weeping" will be determinately true or false in every model, instead of lacking a truth value, as it would in a model in which "Mary" had no reference. In the case of intensional logics, the problem arises that the referent of a name may not exist in some possible worlds. Does the name then *lack* reference in those worlds? This is one way of looking at it. But it has been attacked as involving a subtle mistake. It is one thing, the objection runs, to say that a name refers to something that under different circumstances would not have existed, and quite another to say that under different circumstances the name would not have referred to anything; we are interested not in what it *might* have referred to, but in what it does refer to.[17] Assuming that this is so, what happens to the truth value of "Mary is weeping" in worlds in which Mary does not exist? One possible answer is that it has no truth value in such worlds, because existence is a prerequisite not only for having properties but even for lacking them. Another is that it is false, because an atomic predicate like "is weeping" has in its extension for a given world only things that exist in that world, and is false of everything not in its extension. In the former case, "Mary is either weeping or not weeping" will not be necessarily true, in the sense of being true in all possible worlds. But this can be papered over by defining a necessary truth as one that is not *false* in any possible world. Some such convention seems to be required in order to preserve the rule of necessitation. In the latter case, this logical problem does not arise, though for the essentialist there is the metaphysical one that "necessarily, Mary is human" is now *false*, causing him to do some papering over of his own. Moreover, the decision to treat atomic predicates

---

[17] The objection is due to Kaplan (1973, 503), who also notes that *variables*, at any rate, must be taken as referring to the same thing in all possible worlds, including those in which the thing does not exist.

as false of nonexistents already has an air of convention about it, if only because the distinction between atomic and nonatomic predicates is more or less arbitrary. How can the question whether Mary is dead or alive turn on whether "dead" or "alive" is taken as atomic? By contrast, the decision to treat them as neither true nor false can be defended on metaphysical grounds, whatever problems it may pose for logic. The reason it is not the case that Hecuba is either weeping or not weeping in the actual world is not because "Hecuba" does not refer, but because Hecuba does not exist. It has nothing to do with language. For just the same reason, it is not the case that Mary is either weeping or not weeping in a world in which Mary does not exist. To maintain that it might nevertheless be true, because "Mary" still refers to Mary in such a world, would be to sever the connection between truth and what is the case in exchange for rather paltry gains.

But Davidson's premise derives what plausibility it has precisely from the assumption that logical truths are true in all possible worlds. For if they were, then logically equivalent sentences would be true in exactly the *same* worlds. To be sure, this would not yet mean that they are made true by the same facts. For two facts might be distinct even if neither can exist without the other. In that case, sentence S might be made true by fact F and not by fact G, while sentence T was made true by fact G and not by fact F, even though S and T were true in exactly the same worlds. To rule out this possibility, we should have to assume that facts are identical whenever they necessarily coexist. But this assumption, unlike the one about logical equivalence, can be defended. It is one way of giving cash value to the doctrine that facts are more basic than the things and relations into which we analyze them. For it provides a criterion of identity for facts other than the familiar structuralist one according to which facts are the same if and only if they consist of the same constituents combined in the same way.[18]

The latter criterion really takes the constituents as basic. In order to find out whether the fact that Brutus killed Caesar is the same as the fact that Caesar was killed by Brutus we first have to determine whether there is a relation of being killed by as well as one of killing. And if there is, then

---

[18] The term "structuralist" is due to Fine, who distinguishes between structuralist and "empirical" criteria of identity for a wide range of entities, including facts and propositions. The empirical criterion is so called because entities satisfying it are supposedly empirically distinguishable, empirical distinctions being "ones that make a possible difference to the world." In the case of facts, the relevant criterion is necessary coexistence. I shall call this the "existentialist" instead of the "empirical" criterion, both to avoid the misleading suggestion that it has anything to do with experience and to stick with the Gallic motif introduced by "structuralist."

there are automatically two facts instead of just one. That is, there cannot be two genuinely different *analyses* of a fact, one of which assigns it different constituents from the other, but at most two different *expressions* for it. It seems to me that the existentialist criterion is the one we actually employ. We ask ourselves whether either fact could conceivably exist without the other, and we take a negative answer as showing that they are really one and the same. This criterion also makes good sense of the claim that facts are parts of reality, as opposed to mere aspects. It may be seen as a version of the medieval idea that things are really, as opposed to merely formally, distinct if it is possible, for God at least, to separate them.

The proposed criterion may seem to discard one of the main advantages of facts over possible worlds as a tool of semantic analysis. For it assumes that only those facts exist that can be represented by sets of possible worlds.[19] It has been perceived as a weakness of possible worlds semantics that it is unable to discriminate between necessarily equivalent propositions. The most elementary truth of arithmetic and the most recondite mathematical theorem are both assumed to be true in all possible worlds, and thus to express the same proposition, since the proposition expressed by a sentence is identified with the set of possible worlds in which it is true. Attempts to individuate propositions more finely, such as Carnap's notion of "intensional isomorphism," have generally been adjudged a failure. But by starting from facts, or states of affairs, instead of possible worlds, we may hope to overcome this problem. For since states of affairs are not total like possible worlds, we are free to individuate them as finely as we please. We can distinguish the fact that Brutus killed Caesar from the fact that Caesar was killed by Brutus, or the fact that someone is a bachelor from the fact that he is an unmarried man. And by taking propositions as sets of states of affairs, we can pass the dividends on to them.

Barwise and Perry originally treated propositions in more or less this way as sets of situation *models*. More recently, however, in what they describe as a move in the direction of greater realism, they have abandoned situation models and other set-theoretic constructions for a theory of

---

[19] Which is not, of course, to say that facts *are* sets of possible worlds, or even that possible worlds are anything more than a colorful way of talking about possibility. It may be worth mentioning that not every set of possible worlds represents a fact. First, only those containing the actual world are eligible to do so. Secondly, if we assume that there is no fact that *either* snow is white or the moon is blue, then the set of possible worlds in which this disjunction obtains will not represent a fact either, but only the set of those in which the first *disjunct* does. Thus even within possible worlds semantics there would be room for a distinction between facts and propositions.

situations themselves, their properties, and the relations between them. These properties and relations are not necessarily extensional. On the new theory, two things are needed for a proposition, a situation and a situation type, which is a property of situations. The proposition is true just in case the situation is of the type.[20] Propositions will thus be at least as finely individuated as situation types. But since the latter are not necessarily extensional, they do not depend for their individuation upon situations themselves. The situations themselves can thus be relatively coarsely individuated, as they would be under the existentialist criterion. Hence there is no longer any reason for positing situations beyond necessity.

None of this is of any use to Davidson, of course, since his argument depends, not on the plausible assumption that necessarily coexistent facts are the same, but on the implausible one that logically equivalent sentences correspond to the same fact. Suppose that "S" is "Socrates is an honest man." The former assumption does not imply that the fact that S is the same as the fact that $\iota x(x = \text{Diogenes} \ \& \ S) = \iota x(x = \text{Diogenes})$. These facts do not necessarily coexist, since the latter does not exist in a world unless Diogenes does. Davidson needs the assumption about logical equivalence because his argument turns on a logical trick. But this was not obviously the case with Church's version of the argument, which did not involve smuggling in foreign objects like Diogenes. Although he employed an unexplicated notion of synonymy to establish that his sentences (2) and (3) refer to the same thing, they would seem to be true in the same possible worlds, so that the existentialist criterion could be appealed to instead. Let us consider a more general version of this argument.

Substitutivity and Singular Terms. The remark of Gödel's quoted at the beginning of this chapter appeared in a discussion of Russell's theory of descriptions (196–199). As he saw it, Russell had to give up either the principle of substitutivity or the assumption that descriptions refer to the thing described. For these two principles together imply Frege's conclusion that all true sentences signify the same thing, contrary to Russell's view

---

[20] A situation type is neither true nor false by itself, but only when applied to a situation. For this reason, it is not itself a proposition. According to Perry, we tend to overlook this because we automatically take the relevant situation as the whole world. But this gives unintended results in some cases. For example, "the man with a beard is a philosopher" would normally be understood to apply to some limited situation determined by the context, in which there was only one man with a beard. The view that propositions are properties of facts was first put forward by Baylis, who does not seem to have assumed that every proposition is true or false per se.

that they signify or correspond to many different facts. Gödel does not give the actual argument, but in a footnote he adds:

> The only further assumptions one would need in order to obtain a rigorous proof would be: 1) that "$\phi(a)$" and the proposition "a is the object which has the property ϕ and is identical with a" mean the same thing and 2) that every proposition "speaks about something," i.e., can be brought to the form $\phi(a)$. Furthermore one would have to use the fact that for any two objects a. b. there exists a true proposition of the form $\phi(a, b)$ as, e.g., $a = b$ or $a = a$. $b = b$.[21]

This suggests that he has in mind an argument like the following. Let S and T be any true sentences. Then S can be brought into the form $\phi(a)$ and T can be brought into the form $\psi(b)$, by assumption (2). Let U be any true proposition of the form $\chi(a, b)$. By assumption (1), "$\phi(a)$" signifies the same thing as "$a = \iota x(\phi(x)\ \&\ x = a)$," and "$\chi(a, b)$" signifies the same thing as "$a = \iota x(\chi(x, b)\ \&\ x = a)$." These identities are thus true (assuming that sentences that signify the same thing have the same truth value). Hence, by substitutivity, "$\phi(a)$" signifies the same thing as "$\chi(a, b)$." But by (1), the latter signifies the same thing as "$b = \iota x(\chi(a, x)\ \&\ x = b)$," while "$\psi(b)$" signifies the same thing as "$b = \iota x(\psi(x)\ \&\ x = b)$." Thus by substitutivity again, "$\chi(a, b)$" signifies the same thing as "$\psi(b)$." To summarize, each successive item in the following series signifies the same thing as its predecessor:

$$
\begin{array}{l}
S \\
\phi(a) \\
a = \iota x(\phi(x)\ \&\ x = a) \\
a = \iota x(\chi(x, b)\ \&\ x = a) \\
\chi(a, b) \\
b = \iota x(\chi(a, x)\ \&\ x = b) \\
b = \iota x(\psi(b)\ \&\ x = b) \\
\psi(b) \\
T
\end{array}
$$

Thus by the transitivity of identity, S signifies the same thing as T.

This argument does not rely on the dubious assumption that logically equivalent sentences signify the same thing, employing in its place the

[21] I am not sure whether "mean the same thing" in (1) should be read as a stylistic variant of "signify the same thing" or whether some stronger notion of synonomy is intended. But the former is clearly sufficient for the argument.

weaker assumption (1). But the latter assumption follows from the existentialist criterion of identity for facts. For clearly every possible world in which a has the property ϕ is also one in which a is *the* thing that has ϕ and is identical with a. Assumption (2) might be questioned in the case of generalizations like "$(\exists x)\phi(x)$," but presumably such statements are to be given the Fregean treatment and analyzed as second-order predications.[22] The existence of U is described as a fact rather than an assumption because it is easy to give trivial examples of such a sentence, as Gödel does. To revert to Russell's image in connection with Hegel, U is the hook that grapples a onto b, and the argument presupposes that every "apparently separate piece of reality" is equipped with such hooks. Gödel does not seem to think that (1) and (2) are really open to doubt either, which is why he views the argument as presenting Russell with the above dilemma.

As we all know, Russell chose to give up the assumption that descriptions refer to the thing described. Indeed, he held that they do not refer to anything, but are what he termed "incomplete symbols." Sentences containing them are really abbreviations of other sentences of which no single part can be said to correspond to the description. For example, "Scott is the author of *Waverley*" is an abbreviation of the sentence "one and only one thing wrote *Waverley* and that thing is the same as Scott." This obviously gets around the slingshot, since the latter sentence does not contain "the author of *Waverley*" as a singular term, and so there can be no question of substituting some other singular term for it. But Gödel was not satisfied with this solution. "I cannot help feeling," he said, "that the problem raised by Frege's puzzling conclusion has only been evaded by Russell's theory of descriptions and that there is something behind it which is not yet completely understood." (199)

Barwise and Perry credit Donnellan with having discovered what this something is (1980, D31). According to Donnellan, Frege's and Russell's theories of descriptions should be viewed, not as mutually exclusive alternatives, but as two different ways of *using* descriptions. Someone who asks "Does the pitcher always try to hit the batter?" may be inquiring either about the rules of baseball or about the habits of a particular pitcher, depending on how the definite description is being used. The former use, which Donnellan calls "attributive," corresponds roughly to Russell's theory, while the latter, which he calls "referential," corresponds roughly to Frege's. In situation semantics, this becomes a distinction between two different ways in which the definite description can contribute to the interpretation of statements in which it occurs. On the one hand, it can contribute

---

[22] Throughout the article, Gödel uses lower-case Greek and Roman letters with typical ambiguity, as would have to be the case here.

the object described, in which case that object will be a constituent of every situation in the interpretation. This is called the "value-laden" interpretation, because the description is assigned a particular value; it corresponds to Donnellan's referential use. If, on the other hand, the description contributes the complex of objects and relations in *terms* of which the object is described, it is these and not the object itself that will be constituents of the relevant situations. This is called the "value-free" interpretation, and it corresponds to Donnellan's attributive use.

Armed with this distinction, Barwise and Perry argue that we do not have to give up *either* substitutivity *or* the assumption that descriptions refer to the thing described, provided that we take care to avoid a certain form of equivocation. According to them, the slingshot turns on such an equivocation, and is invalid for that reason. For example, when, in Church's version of the argument, we substitute "the man who wrote twenty-nine Waverley Novels altogether" for "the author of *Waverley*," we are giving both definite descriptions a value-laden interpretation. After all, it is only by taking both expressions as referring to Scott that we are entitled to substitute one for the other in the first place. Similarly, when we substitute "the number of counties in Utah" for "the number such that Scott wrote that many Waverley Novels altogether," we have to take both expressions as standing for twenty-nine. Thus in order to make the steps from sentence (1) to sentence (2) and from (3) to (4) come out right, we have to interpret the first two sentences as standing for the fact that Scott is Scott, a fact whose only constituents are Scott and the relation of identity, and the last two as standing for the fact that twenty-nine is twenty-nine, a fact whose only constituents are twenty-nine and identity. But on this interpretation, (2) and (3) obviously do not stand for the same fact. In order to make them do so, we must exploit the *value-free* interpretation of the definite descriptions, according to which both sentences stand for a fact whose constituents include Scott, twenty-nine, and writing so and so many Waverley Novels altogether. But then the definite descriptions no longer refer to *anything*, let alone to Scott and twenty-nine, and so substitutivity fails to apply. Thus, according to Perry and Barwise, we are free to interpret our descriptions any way we like, so long as we choose one interpretation and stick to it, instead of changing in the middle of an argument.[23]

---

[23] This would have repercussions on Gödel's assumption (1) as well, since in general it is only on the *value-free* interpretation of the description that "$a = \iota x(\phi(x) \,\&\, x = a)$" will signify the same as "$\phi(a)$," even by the modal criterion. For "$\phi(a)$" and "$a = a$" will be true in the same possible worlds only if ϕ is an essential property of a. But see below.

This is a persuasive diagnosis, and the accompanying prescription certainly removes the symptoms. But it relies quite explicitly upon the structuralist criterion, taking it for granted that where there are different constituents there must also be different facts. By a non-structuralist criterion, such as the existentialist one, one and the same fact may well have alternative analyses: one involving the object described by a description, and one involving the complex of objects and relations in terms of which it is described. By the existentialist criterion, this will be true whenever the description necessarily applies to the object in question and to no other. Trivial examples of this kind are easily generated using Gödel's assumption (1) and taking ϕ to be an *essential* property of a. (The reader can decide for himself whether the *structuralist* criterion is even plausible in this case.) But there are also non-trivial examples. For instance, descriptions of numbers in terms of their arithmetic relations to other numbers are presumably of this kind. And, on some views, so are descriptions of ordinary physical objects in terms of their composition or origins. The descriptions used in the slingshot, however, are not. Scott is not *necessarily* the author of *Waverley*, nor is twenty-nine necessarily the number of counties in Utah. Thus the slingshot ought to come out invalid even by the existentialist criterion. But from this point of view, the medicine prescribed by Barwise and Perry is too strong. So long as "$d(a)$" is a description that necessarily applies to b and b alone, we should be able to substitute "$d(a)$" for "b" and then substitute another term for "a," without necessarily affecting the corresponding fact. They would forbid the second substitution on the grounds that by substituting "$d(a)$" for "b" we have given it a value-loaded interpretation, so that the statement is not really about a, appearances to the contrary.

An obvious alternative is to restrict substitution to terms that are not merely coreferential but necessarily so. Something of the sort is often proposed as a cure for the ills of quantified modal logic. These stem from Quine's observation that from the true sentences "necessarily, nine is greater than five" and "nine is the number of planets" we can infer by substitutivity of identity the apparently false one, "necessarily, the number of planets is greater than five." The proposed restriction would block the inference, since "nine" and "the number of planets" do not necessarily refer to the same thing. Opinions differ as to whether this should be formulated as a restriction on substitution into modal contexts (Hintikka) or on what is to count as a singular term (Føllesdal). The former view seems the more attractive for a number of reasons, notably the difficulty of thinking that matters of consequence could turn on what we count as singular terms, but it is exposed to various objections which it would be tedious to go into here. And since Føllesdal has explicitly applied his ideas to the slingshot as well as to the modal case, it will be convenient to go along with his formulation. His remedy is the same in both cases, viz, "a radical purge of the singular terms." (95) Only a subclass of the terms commonly so called should be counted as genuine singular terms, in his opinion, and the rest should be regarded as a species of general terms.[24] Genuine singular terms will be ones that refer to the same object in all possible worlds. In the case of descriptions $\iota x F x$, this means that there must be something that is *necessarily* the only F, as opposed to there just being necessarily *something* that is the only F.[25] Substitutivity, of course, will apply only to genuine singular terms, since the others are not singular terms at all.

This gets around the slingshot, since the definite descriptions it employs do not count as genuine by this criterion.[26] There is some question of motivation, however. In the case of modal logic, the motivation was clear. The problem arose because some terms or purported terms do not refer to the same thing in every possible world. Since in modal logic we are concerned with all possible worlds, we cannot follow our usual practice of substituting such terms for one another just because they happen to have the same reference in the actual world. But the same motivation does not apply in the case of the slingshot, where we are concerned, not with other ways the world might have been, but only with the way it is. A fact is by definition part of the actual world. There is no danger that "the author of *Waverley*" will refer to Manzoni in some other *fact*, as it will in some other possible world.[27] True, there are facts in which Scott does not exist. But

---

[24] They will differ from other general terms in that they will fail to designate unless their extension is a singleton. Presumably the sentence "Scott = the author of *Waverley*" will be ill-formed, since the description is a general term in a position reserved for singular ones.

[25] Føllesdal would really prefer to include *all* definite descriptions in the purge, on the grounds that a singular term should wear its genuineness on its sleeve, as it were, and not just turn out to be genuine. Compare Kaplan (1977, 12): "For me, the intuitive idea is not that of an expression which *turns out* to designate the same object in all possible circumstances, but an expression whose semantical *rules* provide *directly* that the referent in all possible circumstances is fixed to be the actual referent." But Føllesdal himself has vacillated on this. In any case, as noted above, I do not think that the real issue is about singular terms. Besides, it seems perverse to stress the *mechanism* of reference over what is actually referred to.

[26] Gödel's assumption (1) is no longer subject to the objection of footnote 23, since the substitution of "a" for "$\iota x(\phi(x) \mathbin{\&} x = a)$" is now blocked.

[27] As indicated in footnote 20 above, Barwise and Perry hold that the reference of a definite description *can* vary from one situation to another. But not all definite descriptions are of this kind.

if "Scott" occurs in a sentence, all the facts making it true will presumably have Scott, i.e., the author of *Waverley*, as a constituent. Why refrain from substitution? The existential criterion provides an answer of sorts. Indeed, there is an obvious connection between Quine's arguments against modal logic and the slingshot. Quine argued that modal distinctions collapse, i.e., that the only possible world is the actual one. Thus the only sets of possible worlds are the empty set and the set containing just the actual world, which we may identify with Frege's truth values. By the existential criterion, facts are no more finely individuated than (non-empty) sets of possible worlds. So distinctions between facts stand or fall with modal distinctions. But we do not have to invoke the existential distinction explicitly. The reason we cannot substitute "the author of *Waverley*" for "Scott" is not that Scott is not the author of *Waverley*, but that not every fact containing Scott involves him in the writing of *Waverley*. Facts are supposed to be at least partly independent of one another. When we substitute "the author of *Waverley*" for "Scott" in "Scott is Scott," we make use of a fact whose nonexistence is compatible with Scott's being Scott in order to describe the latter fact. This would be harmless if we did not go on to suppose that the describing fact must be part of the fact described.

Since these facts are separate on the structuralist approach as well, the same rationale for not allowing the substitution applies with regard to it. But there is not the same rationale for *allowing* it in cases where the description applies necessarily. Assuming that Scott is necessarily human, "the human being identical with Scott" will be such a description. By the existentialist criterion, we should be able to substitute it for "Scott" without affecting the underlying facts. But on the structuralist approach, Scott's being human will be a separate fact from his being Scott. For this reason, Barwise and Perry's diagnosis seems preferable to Føllesdal's from a structuralist point of view, just as the latter fits the existentialist approach better.

It seems to me that the structuralist approach is exposed to objections of the sort that Bradley made against Russell. For it holds that an object a has the property F if and only if there exists a fact whose constituents are a and F. Bradley's question was what manner of thing a could possibly be. Is it an ordinary thing, replete with all its properties and relations to other things? If so, how can its having F consist in *its* being the constituent of a fact of which F is another constituent? Its identity as a constituent depends on its properties, including F. Moreover, a is supposed to be the same in each of the facts of which it is a constituent. If the fact that a has F is determined by its constituents, and a, which is one of them, has the property G, how can this fact be compatible with a's not being G? It is true that distinct facts can necessarily coexist according to the structuralist. But since G can be *any* property of a, he now appears to be committed to what James called "the Block Universe." Each fact that exists is incompatible with any state of affairs that does not exist. For the state of affairs of a's not being G would have as a constituent a, an object which is G. The structuralist could meet this objection by taking a as a "bare particular," but I do not think that Bradley would be alone in regarding this as a form of theoretical suicide.

The structuralist's model is, of course, the sentence. The *word* "snow" has nothing to do with the word "white." Thus when we say "snow is white" there is no suggestion of redundancy. And when a fact is represented as a *sequence* of objects, it is easy to think of them as words. Wittgenstein once said that it is always analytic to say that one thing is part of another. But that was because he thought that the name of a complex was an *abbreviation* for a description in terms of its parts. Thus when we say that a is part of b what we are really saying is that a is part of the thing whose parts are a and c, whether we are aware of it or not. But this is a possible view only if one is an atomist, and even then it is not necessary. If "b" is not an abbreviation for a description, but rather a *name* of the thing described, the statement that a is part of b is not *analytic*, even if b has these parts essentially. But if we try to form the *fact* that a is part of b we have to put b itself, that is the thing whose essential parts are a and c, into it. The result would be a kind of tautology *in re*. But it seems more than likely that nature abhors such a vacuity. Any theory that posits too close a parallel between language and reality is probably too good to be true.

Bibliography

Anscombe, G. E. M., and Geach, P., 1961. *Three Philosophers.* Oxford: Basil Blackwell.

Aquinas, St. T., 1963. *Commentary on Aristotle's Physics.* Translated by R. J. Blackwell, R. J. Spath, and W. E. Thirlkel. New Haven: Yale University Press.

———, 1964. *Summa Theologiae.* New York: Blackfriars.

Aristotle, 1947. *The Metaphysics.* 2 vols. Translated by H. Tredennick. Loeb Classical Library.

———, 1957. *The Physics.* 2 vols. Translated by P. H. Wicksteed and F. Cornford. Loeb Classical Library.

———, 1961. *Aristoteles Latinus: Categoriae vel Praedicamenta.* Translated by Boethius. Edited by L. Minio-Paluello. Leiden.

———, 1963. *Categories* and *De Interpretatione.* Translated and edited by J. L. Ackrill. Clarendon Aristotle Series. Oxford: Clarendon Press.

Armstrong, D. M., 1978. *Universals and Scientific Realism.* 2 vols. New York: Cambridge University Press.

Augustine, St., 1970. *The Trinity.* Translated by S. McKenna. Washington: Catholic University of America Press.

Austin, J. L., 1961. *Philosophical Papers.* Edited by J. O. Urmson and G. J. Warnock. Oxford: Clarendon Press.

Baker, G. P., and Hacker, P. M. S., 1984. *Frege: Logical Excavations.* New York: Oxford University Press.

Baldwin, J. M., ed., 1901. *Dictionary of Philosophy and Psychology.* 3 vols. New York: Macmillan.

Barwise, J., and Perry, J., 1980. The Situation Underground. In *Stanford Working Papers in Semantics*, edited by J. Barwise and I. A. Sag. Stanford.

————, 1981. Semantic Innocence and Uncompromising Situations. In *Midwest Studies in Philosophy*, Vol. 6, edited by P. A. French, T. E. Uehling, Jr., and H. K. Wettstein. Minneapolis.

————, 1983. *Situations and Attitudes.* Cambridge, MA: M.I.T. Press.

Baylis, C. A., 1948. Facts, Propositions, Exemplification and Truth. *Mind* **57**: 459–79.

Beckmann, J. P., 1967. *Die Relationen der Identitaet und Gleichheit nach J. Duns Scotus.* Bonn: H. Bouvier.

Bergmann, G., 1960. *Meaning and Existence.* Madison: University of Wisconsin Press.

Boler, J. F., 1963. *Charles Peirce and Scholastic Realism.* Seattle: University of Washington Press.

Bradley, F. H., 1899. *Appearance and Reality.* 2nd edtn. New York: MacMillan.

————, 1935. *Collected Essays.* 2 vols. Oxford: Clarendon Press.

————, 1950a. *Essays on Truth and Reality.* Oxford: Clarendon Press.

————, 1950b. *The Principles of Logic.* 2nd edtn. 2 vols. London: Oxford University Press.

Broad, C. D., 1933. *Examination of McTaggart's Philosophy.* 2 vols. Cambridge: Cambridge University Press.

Burge, T., 1984. Frege on Extensions of Concepts, from 1884 to 1903. *Philosophical Review* **93**: 3–34.

Chadwick, J. A., 1927. Logical Constants. *Mind* **36**: 1–11.

Church, A., 1943. Carnap's "Introduction to Semantics." *Philosophical Review* **52**: 298–304.

————, 1956. *Introduction to Mathematical Logic.* Vol. 1. Princeton: Princeton University Press.

Clark, R. L., 1975. Facts, Fact-correlates, and Fact-surrogates. In *Fact, Value, and Perception: Essays in Honor of Charles A. Baylis*, edited by P. Welsh. Durham, NC: Duke University Press.

Davidson, D., 1969. True to the Facts. *Journal of Philosophy* **66**: 748–64.

Donnellan, K., 1966. Reference and Definite Descriptions. *Philosophical Review* **75**: 281–304.

Duns Scotus, J., 1975. *God and Creatures: The Quodlibetal Questions.* Translated and edited by F. Alluntis and A. B. Wolter. Princeton: Princeton University Press.

Eisler, R., 1927. *Woerterbuch der philosophischen Begriffe.* 4th edtn. Berlin: Mittler.

Fine, K., 1982. First-Order Modal Theories III—Facts. *Synthese* **53**: 43–122.

Føllesdal, D., 1983. Situation Semantics and the "Slingshot" Argument. *Erkenntnis* **19**: 91–98.

Frege, G., 1950. *The Foundations of Arithmetic: A logico-mathematical enquiry into the concept of number.* Translated by J. L. Austin. Oxford: Basil Blackwell.

——————, 1964. *The Basic Laws of Arithmetic: Exposition of the System.* Translated and edited by M. Furth. Berkeley: University of California Press.

——————, 1972. *Conceptual Notation and Related Articles.* Translated and edited by T. W. Bynum. Oxford: Clarendon Press.

——————, 1977. *Translations from the Philosophical Writings of Gottlob Frege.* Edited by P. Geach and M. Black. Oxford: Basil Blackwell.

——————, 1979. *Posthumous Writings.* Edited by H. Hermes, F. Kambartel, and F. Kaulbach. Translated by P. Long and R. White. Chicago: University of Chicago Press.

——————, 1980. *Philosophical and Mathematical Correspondence.* Edited by G. Gabriel, H. Hermes, F. Kambartel, C. Thiel, and A. Veraart. Abridged from the German edition by B. McGuinness. Translated by H. Kaal. Chicago: University of Chicago Press.

Geach, P. T., 1972. *Logic Matters.* Berkeley: University of California Press.

Gödel, K., 1972. Russell's Mathematical Logic. In *Bertrand Russell: A Collection of Critical Essays*, edited by D. F. Pears. Garden City, NY: Doubleday Anchor.

Grossmann, R., 1983. *The Categorical Structure of the World.* Bloomington: Indiana University Press.

Hacking, I., 1975. *Why Does Language Matter to Philosophy?* New York: Cambridge University Press.

Hegel, G. W. F., 1977. *Phenomenology of Spirit.* Translated by A. V. Miller. Oxford: Clarendon Press.

Holzer, O., 1951. Zur Beziehungslehre des Doctor Subtilis Johannes Duns Scotus. *Franziskaner Studien* **33**: 22–49.

Horvath, A., 1914. *Metaphysik der Relationen.* Graz.

Kaplan, D., 1973. Bob and Carol and Ted and Alice. In *Approaches to Natural Language: Proceedings of the 1970 Stanford Workshop on Grammar and Semantics*, edited by K. J. J. Hintikka, J. M. E. Moravcsik, and P. Suppes. Dordrecht: Reidel.

————, 1977. *Demonstratives: An Essay on the Semantics, Logic, Metaphysics and Epistemology of Demonstratives and Other Indexicals.* Typescript.

Locke, J., 1974. *An Essay Concerning Human Understanding.* 2 vols. Edited by J. W. Yolton. New York: Everyman.

McTaggart, J. E., 1921. *The Nature of Existence.* 2 vols. Cambridge: Cambridge University Press.

Mill, J., 1878. *Analysis of the Phenomena of the Human Mind.* 2nd edtn. 2 vols. Edited by J. S. Mill. London: Longmans, Green, Reader, and Dyer.

Mill, J. S., 1956. *A System of Logic, Ratiocinative and Inductive.* 8th edtn. London: Longmans, Green and Co.

————, 1961. Autobiography. In *Essential Works of John Stuart Mill*, edited by M. Lerner. New York: Bantam Books.

Moore, G. E., 1899. The Nature of Judgment. *Mind* **8**: 176–93.

————, 1962. *Some Main Problems of Philosophy.* London: George Allen and Unwin.

Ockham, W., 1974. *Ockham's Theory of Terms: Part I of the Summa Logicae.* Translated and edited by M. J. Loux. Notre Dame: University of Notre Dame Press.

————, 1983. *Ordinatio* (Selections). Translated by J. J. Walsh. In *Philosophy in the Middle Ages.* Edited by A. Hyman and J. J. Walsh. Indianapolis: Hackett.

Peirce, C. S., 1931–58. *Collected Papers.* 8 vols. Edited by C. Hartshorne and P. Weiss. Cambridge, MA: Harvard University Press.

Ramsey, F. P., 1950. *The Foundations of Mathematics and other Logical Essays.* Edited by R. B. Braithwaite. London: Routledge and Kegan Paul.

Russell, B., 1906-7. The Nature of Truth. *Proceedings of the Aristotelian Society* n.s. **7**: 28–49.

——————, 1910. Some Explanations in Reply to Mr. Bradley. *Mind* n.s. **19**: 373–8.

——————, 1956. *The Principles of Mathematics.* 2nd edtn. London: George Allen and Unwin.

——————, 1966. *Philosophical Essays.* London: George Allen and Unwin.

——————, 1971. *Logic and Knowledge: Essays 1901-1950.* Edited by R. C. Marsh. New York: Capricorn Books.

——————, 1973. *Essays in Analysis.* Edited by D. Lackey. New York: George Braziller.

——————, 1980. *The Problems of Philosophy.* New York: Oxford University Press.

Sluga, H. D., 1980. *Gottlob Frege.* Boston: Routledge and Kegan Paul.

Vendler, Z., 1967. *Linguistics in Philosophy.* Ithaca: Cornell University Press.

Whitehead, A. N., 1955. *Process and Reality.* New York.

Whitehead, A. N., and Russell, B., 1950. *Principia Mathematica.* 2nd edtn. 3 vols. Cambridge: Cambridge University Press.

Wittgenstein, L., 1974. *Tractatus Logico-Philosophicus.* Translated by D. F. Pears and B. F. McGuinness. 2nd edtn. London: Routledge and Kegan Paul.

Wolter, A. B., 1946. *The Transcendentals and their Function in the Metaphysics of Duns Scotus.* Washington: The Catholic University of America Press.

CSLI Reports

The following titles have been published in the CSLI Reports series. These reports may be obtained from CSLI Publications, Ventura Hall, Stanford University, Stanford, CA 94305.

Research Program on Situated Language. Rep. No. CSLI–84–1. *(NC)*

The Situation in Logic–I. Jon Barwise. Rep. No. CSLI–84–2. *($2.00)*

Coordination and How to Distinguish Categories. Ivan Sag, Gerald Gazdar, Thomas Wasow, and Steven Weisler. Rep. No. CSLI–84–3. *($3.50)*

Belief and Incompleteness. Kurt Konolige. Rep. No. CSLI–84–4. *($4.50)*

Equality, Types, Modules and Generics for Logic Programming. Joseph Goguen and José Meseguer. Rep. No. CSLI–84–5. *($2.50)*

Lessons from Bolzano. Johan van Benthem. Rep. No. CSLI–84–6. *($1.50)*

Self-propagating Search: A Unified Theory of Memory. Pentti Kanerva. Rep. No. CSLI–84–7. *($9.00)*

Reflection and Semantics in LISP. Brian Cantwell Smith. Rep. No. CSLI–84–8. *($2.50)*

The Implementation of Procedurally Reflective Languages. Jim des Rivières and Brian Cantwell Smith. Rep. No. CSLI–84–9. *($3.00)*

Parameterized Programming. Joseph Goguen. Rep. No. CSLI–84–10. *($3.50)*

Morphological Constraints on Scandinavian Tone Accent. Meg Withgott and Per-Kristian Halvorsen. Rep. No. CSLI–84–11. *($2.50)*

Partiality and Nonmonotonicity in Classical Logic. Johan van Benthem. Rep. No. CSLI–84–12. *($2.00)*

Shifting Situations and Shaken Attitudes. Jon Barwise and John Perry. Rep. No. CSLI–84–13. *($4.50)*

Aspectual Classes in Situation Semantics. Robin Cooper. Rep. No. CSLI–85–14-C. *($4.00)*

Completeness of Many-Sorted Equational Logic. Joseph Goguen and José Meseguer. Rep. No. CSLI–84–15. *($2.50)*

Moving the Semantic Fulcrum. Terry Winograd. Rep. No. CSLI–84–17. *($1.50)*

On the Mathematical Properties of Linguistic Theories. C. Raymond Perrault. Rep. No. CSLI–84–18. *($3.00)*

A Simple and Efficient Implementation of Higher-order Functions in LISP. Michael P. Georgeff and Stephen F.Bodnar. Rep. No. CSLI–84–19. *($4.50)*

On the Axiomatization of "if-then-else". Irène Guessarian and José Meseguer. Rep. No. CSLI–85–20. (*$3.00*)

The Situation in Logic–II: Conditionals and Conditional Information. Jon Barwise. Rep. No. CSLI–84–21. (*$3.00*)

Principles of OBJ2. Kokichi Futatsugi, Joseph A. Goguen, Jean-Pierre Jouannaud, and José Meseguer. Rep. No. CSLI–85–22. (*$2.00*)

Querying Logical Databases. Moshe Vardi. Rep. No. CSLI–85–23. (*$1.50*)

Computationally Relevant Properties of Natural Languages and Their Grammar. Gerald Gazdar and Geoff Pullum. Rep. No. CSLI–85–24. (*$3.50*)

An Internal Semantics for Modal Logic: Preliminary Report. Ronald Fagin and Moshe Vardi. Rep. No. CSLI–85–25. (*$2.00*)

The Situation in Logic–III: Situations, Sets and the Axiom of Foundation. Jon Barwise. Rep. No. CSLI–85–26. (*$2.50*)

Semantic Automata. Johan van Benthem. Rep. No. CSLI–85–27. (*$2.50*)

Restrictive and Non-Restrictive Modification. Peter Sells. Rep. No. CSLI–85–28. (*$3.00*)

Equations, Schemata and Situations: A Framework for Linguistic Semantics. Jens Erik Fenstad, Per-Kristian Halvorsen, Tore Langholm, and Johan van Benthem. Rep. No. CSLI–85–29. (*$7.00*)

Institutions: Abstract Model Theory for Computer Science. J. A. Goguen and R. M. Burstall. Rep. No. CSLI–85–30. (*$4.50*)

A Formal Theory of Knowledge and Action. Robert C. Moore. Rep. No. CSLI–85–31. (*$5.50*)

Finite State Morphology: A Review of Koskenniemi (1983). Gerald Gazdar. Rep. No. CSLI–85–32. (*$1.50*)

The Role of Logic in Artificial Intelligence. Robert C. Moore. Rep. No. CSLI–85–33. (*$2.00*)

Applicability of Indexed Grammars to Natural Languages. Gerald Gazdar. Rep. No. CSLI–85–34. (*$2.00*)

Commonsense Summer: Final Report. Jerry R. Hobbs, et al.. Rep. No. CSLI–85–35. (*$12.00*)

Limits of Correctness in Computers. Brian Cantwell Smith. Rep. No. CSLI–85–36. (*$2.50*)

On the Coherence and Structure of Discourse. Jerry R. Hobbs. Rep. No. CSLI–85–37. (*$3.00*)

The Coherence of Incoherent Discourse. Jerry R. Hobbs and Michael H. Agar. Rep. No. CSLI–85–38. (*$2.50*)

The Structures of Discourse Structure. Barbara Grosz and Candace L. Sidner. Rep. No. CSLI-85-39. *($4.50)*

A Complete Type-free, Second-order Logic and its Philosophical Foundations. Christopher Menzel. Rep. No. CSLI-86-40. *($4.50)*

Possible-world Semantics for Autoepistemic Logic. Robert C. Moore. Rep. No. CSLI-85-41. *($2.00)*

Deduction with Many-Sorted Rewrite. José Meseguer and Joseph A. Goguen. Rep. No. CSLI-85-42. *($1.50)*

On Some Formal Properties of Metarules. Hans Uszkoreit and Stanley Peters. Rep. No. CSLI-85-43. *($1.50)*

Language, Mind, and Information. John Perry. Rep. No. CSLI-85-44. *($2.00)*

Is Computation Formal? Brian Cantwell Smith. Rep. No. CSLI-86-45. *(Forthcoming)*

Constraints on Order. Hans Uszkoreit. Rep. No. CSLI-86-46. *($3.00)*

Linear Precedence in Discontinuous Constituents: Complex Fronting in German. Hans Uszkoreit. Rep. No. CSLI-86-47. *($2.50)*

A Compilation of Papers on Unification-Based Grammar Formalisms, Parts I and II. Stuart M. Shieber, Fernando C.N. Pereira, Lauri Karttunen, and Martin Kay. Rep. No. CSLI-86-48. *($4.00)*

An Algorithm for Generating Quantifier Scopings. Jerry R. Hobbs and Stuart M. Shieber. Rep. No. CSLI-86-49. *($2.50)*

Verbs of Change, Causation, and Time. Dorit Abusch. Rep. No. CSLI-86-50. *($2.00)*

Noun-Phrase Interpretation. Mats Rooth. Rep. No. CSLI-86-51. *($2.50)*

Noun Phrases, Generalized Quantifiers and Anaphora. Jon Barwise. Rep. No. CSLI-86-52. *($2.50)*

Circumstantial Attitudes and Benevolent Cognition. John Perry. Rep. No. CSLI-86-53. *($1.50)*

A Study in the Foundations of Programming Methodology: Specifications, Institutions, Charters and Parchments. Joseph A. Goguen and R. M. Burstall. Rep. No. CSLI-86-54. *($2.50)*

Quantifiers in Formal and Natural Languages. Dag Westerståhl. Rep. No. CSLI-86-55. *($7.50)*

Intentionality, Information, and Matter. Ivan Blair. Rep. No. CSLI-86-56. *($3.00)*

Graphs and Grammars. William Marsh. Rep. No. CSLI-86-57. *($2.00)*

Computer Aids for Comparative Dictionaries. Mark Johnson. Rep. No. CSLI–86–58. (*$2.00*)

The Relevance of Computational Linguistics. Lauri Karttunen. Rep. No. CSLI–86–59. (*$2.50*)

Grammatical Hierarchy and Linear Precedence. Ivan A. Sag. Rep. No. CSLI–86–60. (*$3.50*)

D-PATR: A Development Environment for Unification-Based Grammars. Lauri Karttunen. Rep. No. CSLI–86–61. (*$4.00*)

A Sheaf-Theoretic Model of Concurrency. Luís F. Monteiro and Fernando C. N. Pereira. Rep. No. CSLI–86–62. (*$3.00*)

Discourse, Anaphora and Parsing. Mark Johnson. Rep. No. CSLI–86–63. (*$2.00*)

Tarski on Truth and Logical Consequence. John Etchemendy. Rep. No. CSLI–86–64. (*$3.50*)

The LFG Treatment of Discontinuity and The Double Infinitive Construction in Dutch. Mark Johnson. Rep. No. CSLI–86-65. (*$2.50*)

Categorial Unification Grammars. Hans Uszkoreit. Rep. No. CSLI–86-66. (*$2.50*)

Generalized Quantifiers and Plurals. Godehard Link. Rep. No. CSLI–86-67. (*$2.00*)

Radical Lexicalism. Lauri Karttunen. Rep. No. CSLI–86-68. (*$2.50*)

What is Intention? Michael E. Bratman. Rep. No. CSLI–86-69. ()

Understanding Computers and Cognition: Four Reviews and a Response. Mark Stefik, Editor. Rep. No. CSLI–87-70. ()

The Corresponding Continuum. Brian Cantwell Smith. Rep. No. CSLI–87-71. (*$4.00*)

The Role of Propositional Objects of Belief in Action. David J. Israel. Rep. No. CSLI–87-72. ()

From Worlds to Situations. John Perry. Rep. No. CSLI–87-73. ()

Two Replies. Jon Barwise. Rep. No. CSLI–87-74. ()

CSLI Lecture Notes

The titles in this series are distributed by the University of Chicago Press and may be purchased in academic or university bookstores or ordered directly from the distributor at 5801 Ellis Avenue, Chicago, Illinois 60637.

A Manual of Intensional Logic. Johan van Benthem. Lecture Notes No. 1. (*Paper $8.95*)

Emotions and Focus. Helen Fay Nissenbaum. Lecture Notes No. 2. (*Paper $8.95*)

Lectures on Contemporary Syntactic Theories. Peter Sells. Lecture Notes No. 3. (*Paper $11.95 Cloth $23.95*)

An Introduction to Unification-Based Approaches to Grammar. Stuart M. Shieber. Lecture Notes No. 4. (*Paper $8.95 Cloth $17.95*)

The Semantics of Destructive LISP. Ian A. Mason. Lecture Notes No. 5. (*Paper $14.95 Cloth $29.95*)

An Essay on Facts. Ken Olson. Lecture Notes No. 6. (*(Forthcoming)*)

Logics of Time and Computation. Robert Goldblatt. Lecture Notes No. 7. ( )

Word Order and Constituent Structure in German Hans Uszkoreit. Lecture Notes No. 8. (*(Forthcoming)*)

Color and Color Perception: A Study in Anthropocentric Realism David Russel Hilbert. Lecture Notes No. 9. (*(Forthcoming)*)

Prolog and Natural Language Analysis Fernando C.N. Pereira and Stuart M. Shieber. Lecture Notes No. 10. (*(Forthcoming)*)

Lecture Notes on Non-Well-Founded Sets Peter Aczel. Lecture Notes No. 11. (*(Forthcoming)*)

CSLI Lecture Notes report new developments in the study of language, information, and computation. In addition to lecture notes, the series includes monographs and conference proceedings. Our aim is to make new results, ideas, and approaches available as quickly as possible.